BURTON BERNSTEIN

Family
Matters

SAM, JENNIE,
AND
THE KIDS

AN AUTHORS GUILD BACKINPRINT.COM EDITION

Family Matters:
Sam, Jennie, and the Kids
All Rights Reserved © 1982, 2000 by Burton Bernstein

AN AUTHORS GUILD BACKINPRINT.COM EDITION

Published by iUniverse.com, Inc.

For information address:
iUniverse.com, Inc.
5220 S 16th, Ste. 200
Lincoln, NE 68512
www.iuniverse.com

Originally published by Summit Books

Without some of the original illustrations;

revised with a new Epilogue by Burton Bernstein

ISBN: 0-595-13342-8

Printed in the United States of America

For Jennie

Sam
and
Jennie

*T*HERE IS A FAMILY PHOTO-
graph that has hung on one or another of my walls since
early 1962. It is the sort of eight-by-ten glossy that one
would ordinarily file away as a best-forgotten souvenir of,
say, some cousin's wedding or a hazy evening in a Caribbean nightclub—a memento remarkable only for its flashlit
frozen fraction of time and space. Yet this photograph is
dear to me. For some reason, it is the only picture ever
taken of my immediate family and me, all of us together in
one place.

The place was a florid room in Boston's Sheraton Plaza
Hotel, where we had all gathered, decked out in formal
evening dress, just before the grandest moment in my father's life—a testimonial dinner honoring him on his seventieth birthday, tendered by the Boston Lubavitz Yeshiva,
his favorite charity. Actually, his seventieth birthday had
occurred two days earlier, on January 5, 1962, but that date
fell on a Friday, the start of the Jewish Sabbath, and to
hold the "affair" (as it was inevitably called by my parents
and their friends) that night was out of the question. Sunday night was a good compromise—good, too, for the notable Gentiles present: the astonishingly yarmulked Mayor
of Boston, John Collins; the Lieutenant Governor of Massachusetts, Edward McLaughlin; and the State Attorney
General, Edward J. McCormack. Hundreds of disparate

people had turned up at the Sheraton Plaza's main ball-room to honor Mr. Samuel Joseph Bernstein, Boston merchant and civic leader. The fact that his older son, Mr. Leonard Bernstein, would be present as a guest speaker didn't hurt the attendance any.

Seven of us are in that glossy photograph, standing transfixed by the blinding, tyrannical Graflex: five of the immediate family and two daughters-in-law. (The grandchildren were then too young to sit still throughout a grandfather's testimonial dinner.) In the middle, flanked by the sons, the daughter, and the daughters-in-law, are the honored paterfamilias and his wife of more than forty-four years, Jennie Bernstein, née Resnick. Every time the picture catches my eye, I try to puzzle out the peculiar expression on Sam's face. Heady joy is there, certainly, but so is fear, turtlelike fear, as his bald, bespectacled head emerges from his ill-fitting tuxedo jacket. He was always a great worrier, and even this glorious occasion, his very own testimonial, couldn't erase his prime worry. Indeed, it served to heighten it. His prime worry was that he had reached the end of the Biblical span—three score years and ten—and, according to his deepest beliefs, he had no business living any longer. Then, too, he had recently consulted a distinguished doctor at Massachusetts General Hospital about chest pains and what he called "my legs drawing." Before the year was out, the doctor would write him, ". . . you present very definite signs of hardening of the arteries. This is manifested by the chest pain, as well as the discomfort in your leg on walking. I have given you a prescription for nitroglycerin, which I would like to have you take whenever you have any chest tightness. . . . As regards the discomfort in your legs . . . the only real way to overcome this is by surgery." By the spring of 1964, Sam had an aneurysm of the aorta, and surgery was hurriedly called for. His weakened, ballooning aorta was replaced by a new

Orlon one, and it gave him five more years of precarious life.

Jennie is on Sam's left in the picture, his left hand gripping her right elbow. She is dazzled, as she tends to be when in or near the spotlight; she has been in or near the spotlight hundreds of times since November 14, 1943, when Lenny became famous literally overnight, but she has never been at ease with public attention. Her hair has been recently done for the affair, a stiff frame for her fine, strong face. But the sequined harlequin glasses she insists on wearing unfortunately point up her fixed stare, her rigid smile. The rest of her ensemble is black except for white gloves and evening purse—a black satiny dress with a discreet gold pin, and black pumps, squeezed onto those heavy "Resnick" feet. With her high-heeled pumps, she is as tall as her husband.

To their right are Lenny's wife, Felicia, and Lenny. For a man who has been before thousands of cameras, Lenny appears strangely uncomfortable, like a kid waiting to accept a declamation prize from the high-school principal. His right hand is in his trouser pocket, and he may have been shuffling nervously when the flashbulb went off. He would obviously like to be somewhere else at that moment, but he is the stalwart son nevertheless, standing erect and determined to see the evening through. Just as determined is Felicia. beautiful in her finely made white dress and simple jewelry, her eighth month of pregnancy hardly noticeable. In the photograph, as in real life, she gives the impression of aristocratic grandeur despite her small stature. She used to say that it was a trick she had learned as an actress, something to do with one's carriage and expression, the way the neck is extended. The determination notwithstanding, her tension is betrayed by the clawlike clenching of her left hand and by her smile, more crooked than usual—the latter a dead giveaway of unease for those who knew her well. Still, she is brave in what was for her a disagreeable situation. Her bravery is what I remember most about her. Until she died of cancer, in June of 1978, she had an unfair number of occasions to test her bravery, and she always came through, right up to the last ghastly, humiliating moment.

Shirley, my sister, is to the left of Sam and Jennie. She has affected her sultry look, a pose that covers her disquiet when she knows attention is being paid. She is trim, pretty, and immaculately dressed, and she is game. She appears to be the happiest in the photograph except, perhaps, for Ellen, my wife then (we were divorced in 1977), who is standing next to her, their arms about each other's waists. Ellen—blond, tall, clearly not a Bernstein except in name (she is in fact a daughter of Dutch nobility)—is smiling warmly. In spite of some mutual distrust at first, Ellen and my parents grew close over the years, closer than Felicia and my parents ever did. Jennie and Sam often spoke of Ellen as their "other daughter"—a phrase they couldn't bring themselves to use about Felicia. For Ellen, they were gentle surrogate parents, her own being dim memories.

I have probably the bravest face of the lot. As I recall, I had a temperature of a hundred and two degrees, brought on by a vicious case of the flu. But, like Lenny, I am playing the role of the stalwart son. Also like Lenny, I am uncomfortable in my tuxedo, adolescent-looking, my left hand jammed in my trouser pocket—a mirror image of my brother at the other end of the photograph except for my hooded, febrile eyes and drawn countenance. I, too, am to be a guest speaker ("Remarks," the program noted), and I wished only to be in bed, fast asleep. But it was Sam's testimonial, his big night, and no excuses were allowed.

Every so often when I look at the photograph, I am seized by an odd objective curiosity about these people. It is as if the seven of us were somehow somebody else's family. At such moments, I wonder: Where did they come from? How did they get here? Who are they, really? Why do I belong among them? For that matter, what *is* a family? Why is it so damn important to every one of us? Is it a curse or a blessing, or both?

*J*UST AS SAM WAS THE CYNOsure of the photograph and the evening, so he was the essential center of the family, the patriarch. From the perspective of my childhood, he was an Old Testament figure, beardless and slight but a commanding, omniscient presence, especially at the dinner table. I am thinking particularly of the Sunday-afternoon family dinners. Weekday-evening meals were subdued; all conversation came to a halt at precisely 6:45, when Lowell Thomas and the news boomed from a Zenith radio that was a basic fixture in every dining room we inhabited. My mother or the maid would usually bring in dessert from the kitchen just as Lowell Thomas was saying, "So long until tomorrow," and that was that. Sam would grumble about something that had irritated him in the news or at the office, finish his dessert, and retire to his reading chair, in the living room; my mother would retreat to the kitchen; and my siblings (if they were around) and I would scatter to our homework, piano-practicing, or a quick postprandial game of baseball-against-the-steps outside. But on Sunday afternoons everything was different. The large meal—most likely featuring oleaginous soup, nearly inedible roast beef or steak (Jennie's nearly inedible chicken was reserved for Friday nights), stuffed cabbage, potatoes, string or lima beans, and Jell-O, all served with the "good" china and silver on an embroidered tablecloth—was taken at a leisurely tempo, with no radio interruption until Jack Benny at seven o'clock. Up to Jack Benny, nothing special was

scheduled, unless Sam was in a mood for a drive to downtown Boston to see a movie and stage show at the huge
Metropolitan Theatre, or for a spin to Mary Hartigan's, on
the old Route 128, for fresh ice cream, or, if the weather
was good, for a visit to our country house, in Sharon.
There was time at Sunday dinner to consider the weighty
questions.

The midafternoon meals I remember most clearly were
the ones that took place in our Newton house, where we
lived from 1933 to 1941. For most of those years, the whole
family was around; Lenny was at Boston Latin School and
later at Harvard, and Shirley and I were in Newton public
schools. Sam had made it, in spite of the Great Depression,
and he had built a red brick mansion in Post Office Traditional, which matched his dream of economic arrival. He
had concurrently built a small summer cottage near Massapoag Lake, in Sharon, twenty miles to the south. For
much of that Newton period, we had a live-in maid, and so
Jennie was able to sit in on most of the dinner conversation, although she still couldn't restrain herself from trot-
ting in and out of the kitchen to help the maid. At some
point as the meal progressed, Sam would raise both arms
and rock his wrists, as if to adjust his shirt cuffs—his peculiar gesture that usually signalled the start of a discourse
—and then say, "You know . . ." and we'd be off on a
weighty question. The topics for Sunday discussion were
catholic in nature at their outset—Roosevelt, the dumping
of milk, whatever Lenny had learned at school that week—
but they inevitably ended up as Jewish. Sam liked to think
of his intelligence as far-ranging, but in truth only one area
of thought really concerned him—Judaism and its attendant problems. Sometimes this monomania went to memorable extremes: he once referred to Dwight Eisenhower as
"General Eisenberg" and to Adlai Stevenson as "Steve
Adelson." Still, his parochial knowledge was sound. He had
spent his entire life studying the Talmud and scrutinizing

its fine points with noteworthy rabbis and Judaists. And enveloping this Jewishness like a nimbus was his Hasidic background, with the zealous joy it lent to the religion.

The Hasid in him also evoked long, colorful tales of the Old Country. When he was in top form, he would hold forth until my restlessness at the Sunday dinner table gave the other members of the family a good excuse to change the subject or to move on to some more collective activity. We always allowed for his natural exaggeration of events and color, but most of what he told us has been corroborated by relatives and *landsleit*. Harder corroboration is difficult to come by; the methodical destruction of records, mainly by czarist Russians, Nazis, and Communists, has taken care of that. For the most part, what is left is oral history.

Sam's stories often began fairly close to the genealogical beginning. He claimed (with what certitude I could never understand) that we Bernsteins were descended from the Tribe of Benjamin. Perhaps he was attracted to the Biblical lore that Benjamin was the youngest son of Jacob by Rachel and that his name ("Ben Yamin") means "Son of the Right Hand," or the favorite, the luckiest. The Benjamites were outstandingly brave and skillful archers, and they gave Israel its first king, Saul. Their loyalty and trust in God were evidenced by their hurling themselves into the Red Sea during the Exodus while the other tribes stood about warily. And, of course, Benjamin and Bernstein both begin with the letter B. Just as flimsy is the notion, proposed by some scholars, that most Bernsteins are descended from the Tribe of Issachar via the secular name "Ber." Decidedly less charismatic than the Benjamites, the sons of Issachar held little interest for Sam, I suspect. Whatever our tribal roots, if any, the origin of the name "Bernstein" probably came from Diaspora Jews who dealt in amber (the word is German for that substance) or from the migrating wanderers who just happened to pass through the Austrian town of Bernstein, near Vienna. (Several years ago, when Lenny was in Austria conducting the Vienna Philharmonic, he was made an honorary citizen of Bernstein. He was fêted by the town's entire population, and the mayor presented him with some of the local handiwork in amber and an official copy of the Bernstein coat of arms.) Another theory has it that the Ber progenitor became Berko and Berkowitz (Son of Berko) in the eighteenth-century Polish town of Brody. When Prussia, Austria, and Russia carved up Poland, in 1772, "Berkowitz" reappeared as "Bernstein" in some places. The truth is that nobody knows much about this matter.

Sam's preoccupation with family history neatly disregarded the Diaspora and went directly from the Tribe of Benjamin to sixteenth-century Prussia and Poland. According to Sam, our Bernstein (or Ber) ancestors there were rabbis, but not just everyday officiating rabbis. Rather, they were scholars whose main duty it was to study the Scriptures, the Talmud, and the Midrash from dawn to dusk, when they weren't otherwise praying in the synagogue. Wise counsel was offered to the worthy by these Bernstein sages, but only on the higher plane of philosophy. (I can hear Sam now saying his most cherished of all words in his inimitable way—"phil*ah*sephy.") The wives and older children were the breadwinners, since ethereal scholars couldn't be concerned with such mundane matters; the rabbis' studious labors were work enough, holy work. With the advent of modern Hasidism in eighteenth-century Poland, that evangelical set served, if anything, to intensify this pattern of life, with more zeal and emotion. The Hasidic period marked the flowering of culture and religious rededication in Eastern European *shtetl* life, and the Bernsteins were right in the thick of it.

Hasidism coincided with the partitioning of Poland. Without moving an inch, my Bernstein ancestors found themselves residents-in-not-so-good-standing of the Russian Ukraine—specifically, within the Pale of Settlement of Volhynia Province. These suddenly Russian Jews could not live as normal subjects within the Pale, and they could travel outside the zone only under certain severe restrictions. For instance, Jews were generally forbidden residence in the city of Kiev, right in the middle of the Pale, and only those who were merchants of the first guild, educated professionals, military veterans, or accomplished artisans were allowed any freedom to travel. As a result, ninety-four per cent of all Russian Jews were sequestered within the Pale, numbering less than twelve per cent of the entire population in that geographical area. Officially, the reason for these limitations was to protect the Russian peasants from economic enslavement by Jews. But since Jews were restricted from most land ownership, agriculture, and other ordinary pursuits, they were more or less driven into even greater economic activity—peddling, buying and selling, moneylending. The real reasons for the limitations were that the Russian Orthodox Church feared that the Jews would convert the peasants to Judaism (the Pale area contained fewer Russian Orthodox adherents than other parts of Russia) and that, traditionally, Russians disliked Jews—had disliked them ever since the sixth century B.C., when Semites appeared in Georgia after the destruction of the First Temple.

Under the Romanovs, from 1613 to 1917, the fortunes of the Jews had risen and fallen according to the whims and temperaments of individual czars and czarinas. Michael, the founding Romanov, placed Jews on an equal basis with Germans and other foreigners, but then barred them all from Russia. His successor, Alexis I, was similarly erratic. It is said that Peter the Great, who invited talented foreigners into his land, specifically excluded Jews—those "tricksters and cheats," as he purportedly called them. Yet he appointed Baron Shafirov, a baptized Jew, as Chancellor of the Empire. Catherine I issued a ukase ordering the expulsion of all Jews, but the Ukrainians protested that this policy was causing economic ruin. The measure was relaxed, reinstated, and relaxed again under later rulers. The more liberal Catherine II, who reigned during the first partitioning of Poland and consequently inherited more Jews than Russia had bargained for, issued this edict in 1772:

Religious liberty and inviolability of property are hereby granted to all subjects of Russia, and certainly to the Jews also; for the humanitarian principles of her Majesty do not permit the exclusion of the Jews alone from the favors shown to all, so long as they, like faithful subjects, continue to employ themselves as hitherto in commerce and handicrafts, each according to his vocation.

But still the Jews endured local persecution in the *shtetls*, which increasingly isolated them from their Gentile neighbors. The ghetto was institutionalized.

Paul I, Catherine's son, continued her liberal policies, but he had to deal with burgeoning Hasidism and the sometimes violent schism it caused within the Jewish communities between the traditionalists and the evangelists. However, Hasidism further enriched the *shtetl* culture, already full of spirit, art, tragedy, and humanity. With this flowering of the *shtetl* and its persistent insinuation of Jewishness into Russian life, the successive Romanovs were faced with a monumental Jewish Problem. It became their bête noire, and they handled it in typically mercurial ways: Alexander I was suspiciously lenient; Nicholas I was Draconic, drafting laws to convert Jews, destroy their ethnic character, and render them economically harmless—all of which backfired; the tolerant Alexander II was thwarted by the Nihilism and Pan-Slavism movements; Alexander III was medieval in his reactionism, instituting the infamous May Laws, which were designed to force Jews to convert or leave Russia or starve; and Nicholas II, the last of the Romanovs, was oppressive in a wishy-washy way.

An archetypical Pale *shtetl*—linked to the town of Berezdov, in the Ukrainian Province of Volhynia, once the Luck district of Poland—was situated roughly halfway between Kiev and Rovno, on good farmland along a feeder of the Korchyk River. Before the First Partition of Poland, in 1772, it had a Jewish population of two hundred and five, living in forty-nine houses, but the Jewish population decreased to as few as eighty-seven, following the trend for Jewish residents of the Luck District. By 1847, it was part of the Russian Ukraine, and in spite of the severe rule of Nicholas I, the *shtetl*—called Beresdiv in the Yiddish dialect—had grown to three hundred and eighty-four men and three hundred and ninety women.

One of those Beresdiv men—actually a child in 1847—was Bezalel Bernstein, my paternal great-grandfather, after whom I'm named. ("Burton," of Teutonic origin, is a totally inaccurate Anglicization of "Bezalel;" the former means "bright raven," and the latter, the name of the chief architect of the Tabernacle, is Hebrew for "under the protection of God." About all they have in common is that they both begin with B, like Benjamin and Bernstein.) I am particularly proud of being named after this oldest clearly identifiable ancestor in my father's line, because he was a local legend in life and in death. Departing radically from the usual occupation of Bernstein males before him—that of the sedentary scholar-rabbi—Bezalel, who grew to be a man of height and heft, became a blacksmith. He was an adroit, fearless, straightforward fellow, which resulted in his attracting a large clientele of both Jews and Gentiles from the province. He took a young Jewish woman for a wife, fathered four sons, and prospered by his own sweat. According to what my father had been told, Bezalel could lift up the side of a droshky and, without faltering, remove one of the wheels before setting it down. People would stand around his shop just to watch him perform the feat. He worshipped his God diligently, drank vodka with the kulaks, stood up to any insult, and guaranteed all his good work with his good word—the stuff of legend, and all the more so for a Jew in Volhynia.

But, for all his vital days, it was his death that was re-counted around the hearths and samovars in later years. When Bezalel was in his thirties, he was awakened one night with the news that his blacksmith shop was burning uncontrollably. Barefoot and clothed in only a blanket (so the story goes), he raced out into the winter night, doused himself with a pail of water, and walked into the flaming shop. This mad giant of a man emerged several minutes later dragging his most prized possession—an iron tool chest, glowing red from the fire. Then he collapsed over the chest, dead from the herculean rescue. I like to think that his funeral was attended by dozens of different people from as far away as Kiev, and that they all went off to a tavern and got drunk together afterward. Maybe. Maybe not.

One of the orphan sons he left in the cold world of the Ukraine was Yehuda ben Bezalel—known as Yudel in Yiddish—who at his father's death was about twelve years old. He stayed with his impoverished mother in Beresdiv, while his brothers were sent to live with relatives in neighboring towns. Perhaps because of the manner of his father's death (and his life), Yudel was attracted to the old ways of Bernstein males. He studied diligently and passionately at the local yeshiva, wrapped himself for protection in Hasidism, Talmud, and Torah, and grew up to become another scholar-rabbi—his slight, flaccid body hunched over his books, rocking more or less constantly to the rhythms of devout prayer. He cultivated a beard and long sidelocks. He wore a black caftan and a fur hat—the uniform of the ultra-Orthodox. He knew and cared little for the world beyond the walls of his room, the yeshiva, and the synagogue.

Sam and Jennie

Yet, ultimately, he needed a proper wife (even scholar-rabbis needed wives, or there wouldn't be any new scholar-rabbis), and so a marriage was arranged with a girl from the nearby, larger town of Korets. Her name was Dinah Malamud, and by all accounts she was lovely: blond, blue-eyed, delicate in build and features, gentle, and obliging. Best of all, she was willing to be a scholar-rabbi's wife; which is to say, willing to plow fields, milk cows, grow and prepare food, bear and care for children, and bring in some money while her husband prayed and studied.

Dinah had two brothers, Herschel and Shlomo, and the three were supported throughout most of their childhood by their sturdy, industrious mother, Hilda, for their father had died when they were very young. Hilda, who worked day and night as a candlemaker, was only too happy to marry off her sole daughter at seventeen—and to an intellectual, a yeshiva graduate, a man of God, at that. Of course, it meant that Dinah would be doing all the hard work, but hard work was the rule for a poor Korets girl. Korets was a market town on the banks of the Korchyk, noted mainly for its deposits of kaolin, a fine clay used in porcelain manufacturing. Some photographs I have seen of turn-of-the-century Korets show a wide main street of three-story wooden buildings and thatch-roofed houses, with babushkaed ladies and roughly garbed men leaning out of windows or chatting on a wooden sidewalk. At the time the photographs were taken, ten thousand Jews lived in the *shtetl* sector of the town, and two thousand Gentiles, mostly peasants, lived close by. Once a week, on market day, the Gentiles and the Jews would meet and mix—the Jews selling goods and services to the Gentiles, the Gentiles selling produce and livestock to the Jews. It was a generally peaceful and reciprocally advantageous arrangement. Occasionally, the peace would be disrupted by organized pogroms or spontaneous accusations, either true or fictitious, against Jewish shopkeepers.

Dinah set up a household ten miles down the road in Beresdiv, where her new husband lived. It turned out that she was just as tough, industrious, and willful as her mother, Hilda. By the time she had become a bride, in 1891, Beresdiv was a diminutive version of neighboring Korets. It had a population of more than two thousand, half of whom were Jewish, the others being either Russian Orthodox or Roman Catholic (a reminder of the village's Polish days). There were wheat fields, stores, even a distillery and a brick factory, and some Jews had small farms just outside the *shtetl* proper. On such a farm, rented from a kulak landlord, Dinah and Yudel made a home: a large shack for a house, a barn for a cow and chickens, and an adjacent field big enough to warrant a plow and a workhorse. While Yudel lost himself in his books and prayers, Dinah set to work plowing the field, sowing seed, cooking meals, milking the cow, collecting eggs, and, to bring in a few steady kopecks, making Sabbath candles for the Jews and round loaves of Russian rye bread for the Gentiles. If her delicate frame belied her strength, her hands betrayed it—large, gnarled, and callused, the hands of a good peasant woman. She and Yudel found time to make babies.

*T*HEIR FIRST-BORN CHILD WAS a boy, Yisroel Yosef ben Yehuda, who came into the world in the middle of the Russian winter, on January 5, 1892, delivered by a midwife. Before the circumcision, his first name was changed to Shmuel, for unknown reasons, and he was thereafter called Shmuel Yosef. His own father performed the circumcision rite (Yudel could, when the cupboard was bare, function as an everyday rabbi, although he disliked such prosaic duties), and his mother soon returned to her chores, her infant wrapped at her breast. The year of my father's birth was a grim one for Russian Jews. Earlier liberalizations—such as permitting certain Jews to live beyond the Pale, and even to take part in local governments—were reversed by the despotic Alexander III, and while no major pogroms were recorded in the Beresdiv area during that year, Gentile-Jewish animosity could erupt into violence over a matter as small as a rise in the price of soap.

When Shmuel Yosef was old enough to remember events (and he remembered well, as my childhood Sunday dinners attested), he developed a strange love-hate for his days in Beresdiv. As I gathered from his stories, every pleasant element of that existence had a disagreeable side. For instance, he loved farm life. He would talk with rapture about the smell and warmth of a cow's stall on a freezing day; the unique taste of an egg snatched from under a hen, punctured at both ends, and then sucked dry for an instant breakfast; his delight at plucking a fresh cucumber and eating it unpeeled, with a little salt; the simple sport of stick-hurling, a primitive variant of horseshoes. And yet he abhorred the dumb, monotonous routine of the farm—leading animals to pasture and then bringing them in again; wrestling with stubborn horses (his earliest memory was of being kicked in the head by a horse that he was trying to coax across a stream); dodging the filth and flies of a barnyard. This ambivalence spread to his view of the farmer himself. The peasant farmer to him was a good man, a man of the earth who earned his food by his own toil. (This sentiment would carry over in later years to his attitude about the "Yankees," a broad category in his mind comprising day laborers in Sharon and Brahmin competitors in Boston—in other words, non-Jewish non-immigrants.) He admired the heartiness, the backslapping crudities, the capacity for food, sex, alcohol. But, then, the peasant farmer (or "Yankee") was to him also a dullard, an insensitive boor, a bigot, who was most concerned with brawling or fornicating (or, in the case of certain "Yankees," playing golf at an exclusive country club).

Shmuel Yosef's most pronounced love-hate paradox was toward his parents' manner of living and their religion. While he respected his father's keen mind and lofty position in the community, he was outraged as a child by the cloistered, narrow, downright unhealthy life that Yudel led. Outrageous, too, was his father's custom of studying books and praying all day when the menial work of making a living and raising a family was left to his mother, whose passive acceptance of this situation was at once admirable and infuriating. The Orthodox Hasidic religion that they followed covered Shmuel Yosef's youth like a heavy garment, both protective and suffocating. Judaism entered into every cranny of daily life: no question was too small to be answered by one religious dictum or another; no rite was too inconsequential to be piously observed and mulled over; no sin against God, some of them more local lore than Mosaic law, was too trifling to go unpunished. (My father once told me that he had received a sharp beating at the hands of Yudel for allowing his skullcap to slip off his head during an evening prayer.) And it hardly escaped Shmuel Yosef's notice that this pervading Jewishness was the source of his inferiority and poverty in that inhospitable land.

Still, in the contradictory pattern that dogged him for his entire life, he immersed himself in his religion, drawing succor and joy from it. The Hasidic excesses—the soul-stirring songs, the ecstatic dancing, the arcane mysticism —transported him and, upon reflection in his later years, made living in Russia bearable. He did well in *heder*, a purely religious primary school, fulfilling the promise of the first son of Rabbi Yudel Bernstein. As a rule, Jewish children did not attend secular schools in the small towns within the Pale; secular education was distrusted by the

provincial Orthodox, and government-run schools required all students to perform written work on Saturdays—
an abomination under Jewish law. The *heder* was the answer for the compulsively literate *shtetl* dwellers, the People of the Book. In its standard form at that time, the *heder*
was in the house of the teacher, the *malamud*, who conducted classes for boys of all ages. (Girls could sometimes
listen in on the fringes, but could not take part formally.)
The teacher would instruct just a few children at a time
while the others read aloud or repeated their lessons by
rote. School sessions lasted most of the day, six days a
week, with little or no summer vacation. Discipline was
often brutish, but in such educational anarchy no more
efficient system was possible. Worse still, basically healthy
children were browbeaten into wan, spindly versions of
their elders. Shmuel Yosef recited his lessons, earned his
share of knuckle raps from the *malamud*, and, entertaining
thoughts of becoming a rabbi in the family tradition, he
went on to the town's yeshiva. But for the rest of his days,
as much as he promoted and respected Orthodox Jewish
education (after all, the Boston Lubavitz Yeshiva was his
special charity), he had doubts, sometimes bordering on
contempt, about the sallow, thin products the Orthodox
heder and yeshiva turned out. There was something in him
that wanted these Jewish children to be more like "Yankees."

The family custom in the *shtetl* of those years was to
produce another child approximately every two years, with
the resigned acceptance that the Angel of Death would
take as many as half of them through disease, accident, or
plague. Accordingly, Dinah Bernstein delivered a daughter, Khaye, two years after Shmuel Yosef was born. Two
more children died in infancy, and in the ensuing biennial
intervals there arrived, in 1900, a daughter named Sura-
Rivka; then another victim of untimely death; and, in 1905,
a robust son (perhaps a throwback to Bezalel, the black-

smith) called Shlomo. The surviving children were as
happy as their poverty and strict family life allowed, but as
they matured, all of them—with the exception of Sura-
Rivka—yearned for a common goal: to leave the *shtetl* and
discover a better life somewhere else.

My father once told me that his watershed moment of
decision came just after his bar mitzvah, when he was
thirteen. Even though he was a promising student and a
profoundly religious young man who planned to be a
scholar-rabbi, several forces contrived to make him rebel
and escape. Blood accusations—those vicious, calumnious
rumors that Jews had drained a Christian child's blood for
ritual purposes—were rife in the Ukraine then, and anti-
Semitic upheavals inevitably followed them. While no full-
fledged pogroms struck Beresdiv, several aftershocks were
felt. Nightriders—usually local peasants who had dealt
amiably with the Jews just a few hours before—would gal-
lop into the *shtetl* and smash windows, set fires, and terror-
ize the population. Occasionally, injuries or deaths would
occur. Once, it was said that a unit of Russian soldiers
would be bivouacked near the town and all the Jewish girls
over twelve would be raped. The girls were spirited away to
relatives and friends far from Beresdiv, but the soldiers
never came. The participation of many young urban Jews
in the budding Socialist movement served to increase gov-
ernment-encouraged hostility. And with the outbreak of
the Russo-Japanese War, in 1904, the government grew
desperate for recruits. Jews had long been discriminated
against in the czarist conscription; they were compelled to
supply ten male conscripts per thousand of their population, as opposed to the Christians' seven per thousand, and
to furnish one extra conscript for every thousand rubles in
tax arrearage. The wartime drive to swell the ranks of private soldiers in the Far East reached the teen-agers in
Ukrainian *shtetls*, and Shmuel Yosef was approaching conscription age. Another reason for rebellion and escape was

the continuing strident poverty on the little farm: less food, higher taxes, more mouths to feed. Boarders were taken in, and while Yudel studied and prayed, Dinah and her older son staggered under the heavier work load. Soon, Shmuel Yosef began to hatch plans for fleeing.

The options open for a potential *shtetl* escapee were few. There was the dream of America—the *"Goldene Medina"* ("Golden Country")—and there were the less propitious reveries of Latin America or South Africa, where, some claimed, the immigration of Jews was permitted, even desired. A shorter trek to another European country was simply asking for more trouble; a poor Jew was not welcome anywhere on the Continent. A patently crazy idea, especially in the mind of the rural Russian Jew, was Palestine. Zionism and the agricultural colonization of a desert or a malarial swamp administered by the Ottoman Empire attracted only the most daring and foolhardy in those formative days of Jewish nationalism. For most, including Shmuel Yosef, the Holy Land was still a Biblical vision, to be prayed for and revered but not necessarily to be settled. Running off to join the Russian Socialists was a fascinating possibility, but the escapee had to be willing to renounce his religion and mores, live in hiding for much of the time, and be prepared to face a czarist firing squad. The enterprising majority of restless *shtetl* dwellers chose to strike out for the land of golden promise. Indeed, during the last two decades of the nineteenth century, more than a million Jews left Russia for the United States. In 1903, almost fifty-two thousand attempted that long voyage.

One of those voyagers in 1903 was an adventurous teen-aged lad named Herschel Malamud, Dinah's younger brother and Shmuel Yosef's uncle, who fled Korets one step ahead of the czar's recruiters. He was not many years older than Shmuel Yosef, and his abrupt departure had a telling effect on his nephew. Shmuel walked to Korets and asked those who had helped Herschel escape about the procedure—how to steal across the border to Prussia and Danzig, how to get in touch with the United Hebrew Charities for steerage money to America, how to make do once he arrived there. The Korets people were sympathetic to Shmuel. When a letter came to the Malamuds from Herschel stating that he was living in a Connecticut city called Hartford and was learning the trade of a barber, Shmuel's desire to leave was overwhelming. Dinah learned of his plans, and she absolutely refused to let him go. As the older son, he belonged at home, helping them to exist. Later, he would be a scholar-rabbi, like his father. What was there for him in America? Nothing but savages and wild animals. He wouldn't get as far as Danzig. And even if he did the ocean would swallow him up. Her brother Herschel was lucky; her son wouldn't be so lucky. But the more she forbade it, the more he was determined to leave.

Finally, in 1908, another letter from Uncle Herschel arrived in Korets, and this one contained some money for sixteen-year-old Shmuel—enough to get him to Danzig and perhaps on a ship. Shmuel packed a few pieces of clothing in a blanket roll, and, before he slipped away from the little Beresdiv farmhouse, he said goodbye to his brother and his sisters. Khaye made him promise to send her money from America so that she could leave soon, too. Shlomo, only three at the time, broke down and cried, begging Shmuel to take him along. It wasn't possible. Shmuel would have a hard enough time travelling alone. Sura-Rivka was also too young to understand fully what was happening, but she cried with Shlomo. Frightened and guilty, Shmuel never said goodbye to his parents. He went off to Korets, where he stayed overnight in the Malamud house. Abraham Malamud, Shmuel's first cousin and just eight years old then, has recalled recently how Shmuel arrived at the Korets house and asked to be hidden from his mother and father until he could head west for the border. "He couldn't stand it, living at home," Abraham has said. 'It was a prison for him. They wouldn't let him live, so he ran away." Fifty years later, when my father was once eulogizing life in the Old Country, I asked him why, if it was all so colorful and inspiring, did he leave? I remember that he stared at me as if I were mad.

Travelling at night, Shmuel left Korets on foot for the city of Rovno, about forty miles to the west. Some boiled potatoes, bread, and salt, which he had been given by the Malamuds, kept him going, and a lucky encounter with a Jewish teamster made his passage easier on the swing north toward Warsaw and Danzig. At some point along that route, he joined a group of fellow-emigrants—men, women, and children—who were also heading for Danzig but wanted to skirt Warsaw, to avoid trouble. Danzig, a large port on the Baltic Sea, was then the capital of West Prussia, and so many emigrants of all stripes were crowding into the city that customs observances were chaotic. The wandering band bought food from peasants along the way and took care of one another. Every one of them was going to America.

In Danzig (the biggest city by far that Shmuel had ever seen), he bought a steerage ticket on a coastal steamer that would ultimately call at Liverpool. A representative of the United Hebrew Charities told him that in Liverpool arrangements could be made to advance him money for steerage passage to New York City. Shmuel was worried that he would never be able to leave Liverpool—or, even worse, he would be stranded en route in Kiel or Rotterdam. Conditions in steerage were, at best, hideous, and he began to doubt that he had done the right thing. The weather in the Baltic and the North Sea was typically rough, the passengers were sick, and vermin were everywhere. But at last the ship did dock at Liverpool, where, as promised, a helpful man provided the huddled masses with some vegetable soup, a warehouse to sleep in, and travellers' aid.

What my father remembered most vividly about the last

and longest leg of his escape to America was the awful filth of the steerage hold. He never knew the name of the transatlantic ship—the steerage passengers were simply herded into the dark, forbidding vessel one night—but he could describe in terrifying detail every species of rotten food, excrement, and bug he had encountered during the two-week voyage. His experience in that wretched hold would have a traumatic, lifelong effect on him: dirt, filth, bugs were the enemy, and while they appeared with no more frequency in our household than in any others, he would go on periodic cleanliness tears to eradicate the slightest suggestion of faulty hygiene. He quite happily left the housekeeping chores to my mother, my sister, and our various maids, but every so often he would espy some spilled food in the refrigerator or some ants in the pantry. Then, hot-eyed and possessed, he would shout as if in triumph and begin to scrub the refrigerator or the pantry by himself. Since he had little skill in such matters, he ended up making a greater mess—more spilled food and lusher nesting places for ants—but at least he had proved his point, that filth and vermin were everywhere and that the battle against them must never cease.

On several of these crusades, Sam waged war against cobwebs, which he viewed as repositories for all kinds of germs as well as dead insects. If he spotted a cobweb in even the most inaccessible place, he would go to any pains to remove it, climbing onto tables, mounting ladders, swiping at them with brooms. He referred to these menaces, in his delightfully idiosyncratic English, as "cow-webs," and until I was about six years old I firmly belived that these fine, gossamer configurations were somehow the products of cows, which spun them while we slept at night. Perhaps his oddest act of antisepsis was never allowing a slightly smudged towel to hang from its holder and be used by an unsuspecting victim. Smudged towels, in his mind, were unquestionably the source of whatever ailment he suffered from at any given moment—a head cold, an upset stomach, even his "legs drawing." He was known to fly into a rage at the mere sight of an offending towel, and to accuse my mother of undermining the family's health. But even in his wildest cleanliness rages we understood the reason for them, once we had heard the stories of the transatlantic crossing in 1908.

All my father ever told me about his arrival at the United States Immigrant Station at Ellis Island, in New York Harbor, was that it was crowded, confusing, and cruel. Sick and unsponsored immigrants were summarily held in detention and threatened with deportation; fear and rumor were as abundant as the lice. The motley people hung together, however, and helped one another as they never had before and probably never would again. That, at least, was uplifting and something of a welcome. Luckily, Uncle Herschel was on hand to meet his nephew Shmuel Yosef and to post the twenty-five dollars necessary for sponsorship. With that stroke of good fortune and an Anglicized name supplied by an immigration clerk, Samuel Joseph Bernstein arrived in America.

The uncle's name had also changed, from Herschel Malamud to Harry Levy—"Harry Levy" presumably being easier for his Hartford barbershop customers to pronounce. He had that very year taken a pretty young bride, the former Polly Kleiman, of Hartford, with whom he would live in marital, if childless, bliss until his death, in 1948. (They were the most contented, loving couple I have ever known, the reason being, I suspect, that they lavished the affection and care on each other that ordinarily would have gone to their children, if they could have had them.) With his new responsibilities and his struggling barbershop, Harry Levy was not yet flush enough to take on hired help—namely, his nephew Sam, the greenest of greenhorns. So Harry led the undernourished lad to the likeliest place for a non-English-speaking, unskilled immigrant just off the boat to start his climb up the American ladder—across Manhattan to the Fulton Fish Market. Harry himself had served some time at the fish-cleaning tables there several years before, when he had just got off the boat.

The rank, slimy sheds along the South Street docks were the first stop for thousands of confused immigrant men from all over the world, who were simply handed knives, scalers, and shears and told to clean fish, no questions asked. The way my father described it (and he luxuriated in the telling), gangs of about ten men were posted around large metal-topped tables, each of which was under a chute. Thunder from inside the chute signalled the imminent arrival on the table of an avalanche of sneering fresh fish—bass, flounder, cod, herring, mackerel, and an occasional starfish or other inedible that had slipped by the sorters on the docks—and with that splashy arrival the men would attack. They cleaned, trimmed, and scaled, cleaned, trimmed, and scaled, tossing the carcasses into appropriate ice-filled bins, which other drudges hauled away. (The haulers and the sorters were a cut above the cleaners, being greenhorns a little less green.) Just when the cleaners were handling their last fish each—their skin, hair, and clothes permeated with fish blood, guts, and offal, their feet awash in similar slubber—someone would hose down the table, the thunder would sound again, and another deluge of fish would tumble upon them. So it went from 6 A.M. to 6 P.M., six days out of seven, including Saturday, the Jewish Sabbath—all for five dollars a week plus a cut rate on schmaltz herring for lunch. (Sam existed on herring and black bread.) No holidays. No vacations.

It was backbreaking work, especially for a thin, sixteen-year-old ex-yeshiva student from Beresdiv. In fact, it was gruelling for some of Sam's burly Irish, Italian, and Slavic tablemates. Of these multifarious fellows, Sam claimed that, at one time or another, Al Smith and Leon Trotsky passed through the fish-cleaning rooms, but I have found no supporting evidence for that part of his story. Perhaps they just visited. A far more likely tale concerned a Polish tablemate named Ted, who worked beside my father for a few months. They became fairly friendly, communicating in bits of basic Russian and whatever English they had picked up. They talked of the Old Country, politics, religion, the immigrant's lot. Then, one day, Ted disappeared. About forty years later, my father was sitting in his office, in downtown Boston, talking on the telephone and looking out the window. A window-washer moved along the outside ledge, strapped himself in opposite Sam's gaze, and proceeded to squeegee the glass. The two men stared at each other for a long time, until my father gestured for him to come inside the office through the window. He was, of course, Ted, and they renewed their friendship over lunch at Thompson's Spa, where Sam invariably had the businessman's special every business day. Ted, my father reported, felt uncomfortable in the stiff, pristine, white-tiled restaurant—a "Yankee" spot if there ever was one, with all those bankers, lawyers, and merchants. They parted after lunch, and Sam never heard from Ted again, although they exchanged addresses and promised to keep in touch. "Maybe it was for the best," Sam said. "He didn't feel right with me after the Fulton Fish Market."

Sam liked to call the Fulton Fish Market "my university." There was that certain arrogance of the self-made man implicit in the expression (the "I-went-to-the-College-of-Hard-Knocks" sort of thing), but in many ways he was right. At the glutinous fish-cleaning tables, he learned something approximating English; he heard feverish arguments for the Democrats, the Socialists, and the Anarchists; he realized that he was no worse or better off than the other poor greenhorns; and—the most important lesson of all—he discovered that anything could happen in this America. (He also learned how to clean fish as deftly as any man alive. Whenever we caught a bass or a pickerel in Sharon's Massapoag Lake, I was astounded at how neatly and swiftly he could eviscerate and scale it—tasks he performed with a glee curious in a man with a weak stomach and a dread of dirt.)

On the pungent, swarming lower East Side, where he lived at first in a rented curtained-off segment of a squalid tenement room, he was educated in other matters: how to live on five dollars a week (a dollar and a half for the piece of room, two dollars for food, fifty cents for clothes and sundries, and, without fail, a dollar under the mattress for savings); how to advance oneself through English lessons given at a workingmen's circle, along with a dose of left-wing politics; how to keep his religion alive in the tiny Orthodox synagogues on every street; how to make friends and influence people. His lodgings were owned by some *landsleit* from the Korets-Beresdiv area, and the tenants were constantly changing. A new immigrant would turn up, get a job, and, before long, move on, perhaps to exotic Brooklyn or the Bronx, or even the untamed land across the Hudson River. The rented bed would barely be cool before an even newer immigrant would claim it. There were some good times to be had on Sunday—a balcony seat (for a few pennies) in a Yiddish theatre, or a stroll through the happy clamor and enticing smells of the street.

When Sam heard about a larger, more private room available across the bridge, in the Williamsburg section of Brooklyn, where some distant relatives lived, he moved. In Brooklyn, Sam fell in love. He met a dark-haired girl ("so pretty and beautiful" was how he described her), and he wooed her attentively. She liked to ride in horsedrawn carriages, and Sam obliged, spending a reckless amount of money on her fancy. How far their relationship progressed, how serious their intentions were I have never been able to find out, even when he was in a nostalgic mood and seemed to want to talk about her. I once asked him the big question about the Mysterious Lady, as I had come to think of her: Was she Jewish? He refused to say, which I guess was an answer. From faded photographs of Sam as a young man, I can imagine his having had some success with the Mysterious Lady. He was short but wiry, his muscles toned by long, hard labor, and with his wavy auburn hair, his hazel eyes (unfortunately encircled by store-bought spectacles), and his strong features, he was not a bad-looking fellow—somebody with a future, perhaps.

Sam's ideal concept of the immediate future, in the first two years of his American residency, was to win a solid civil-service position. He had long before observed that in Russia, though there were good times and bad for farmers, landowners, and professionals, one occupational group always seemed to be secure and well fed—the bureaucrats, the civil servants. Both in the Old Country and the New, he had been particularly impressed by the postman, a functionary who commanded respect from everyone, was eagerly awaited each day, and provided an important service. So Sam spent as many hours as he could spare studying English in order to pass the Post Office's examination for an appointment as a letter carrier. In those days, political pull helped in gaining such appointments, but even if Sam had had the pull he wouldn't have had the job. He failed miserably at spelling (a lifelong deficiency) each time he took the examination, although he did well on the mathematics part of the test. Finally, he gave up his goal of becoming a postman. As things turned out, that was a stroke of luck.

Before Passover in the spring of 1912—when Sam was thoroughly depressed by the cheerless toil at the fish-cleaning tables and by his failure as a potential postman—he received a letter from Uncle Harry inviting him to come to Hartford to celebrate the Seder. Harry also suggested that Sam might want to come to Hartford permanently, to work in his barbershop, which had successfully expanded into women's wigs and switches. Sam jumped at the chance and took the train from New York to Hartford. He started at the bottom in Harry's shop, sweeping up hair clippings and sterilizing combs and scissors. It was certainly easier and better-paying work than cleaning fish, but it seemed to hold no future for him, since he hadn't the least inclination or talent to become a cutter of hair, like his uncle. But living in Hartford was pleasant. He was among family—the Kleiman clan that Harry had married into was large and gregarious—and there were good times and plenty to eat. Hartford was also a handsome cultural center, which could boast of a literary tradition including Mark Twain and Charles Dudley Warner, although Sam saw nothing of that rarefied world. In time, he grew restless.

One day, a salesman from the New York firm of Frankel & Smith, purveyors of barber and beauty supplies, paid his regular call on Harry Levy's shop. He mentioned that the company's new Boston branch office was looking for an industrious young man to work as a stockboy. Advancement was possible if the young man was industrious enough. The salesman said that he had noticed Sam's attentiveness to his chores, and he thought that Sam might be a likely candidate. Harry wanted his nephew to stay in Hartford, among family, but Sam had other plans. He took the train to Boston and got the job.

The Edward E. Tower Company, founded in 1861, was the class of the New England barber-and-beauty-supplies business, but the Boston branch of Frankel & Smith was a comer, especially in the category of hair goods. The Frankel brothers—Berthold, Max, and Milton—weren't above taking advantage of a young greenhorn who needed a decent job. By Sam's account, he worked about as hard at the offices of Frankel & Smith, on Summer Street in downtown Boston, as he had at the fish market, and he wasn't paid much more. It was muscle labor, mostly—lifting boxes, sweeping up, cleaning shelves. Occasionally, he would be asked to help sort out hanks of human hair, imported by the firm from European and Oriental dealers who paid impoverished foreign women a pittance for their shorn locks. The hair was then treated chemically and woven into wigs and switches for more solvent, and fashionable, American ladies. The Frankels were second-generation German Jews, well Americanized, and they had no particular sympathy for their Russian immigrant co-religionist. In fact, given the sense of embarrassment "cultured" German Jews felt for Russian and Polish Jews then, it was surprising that they agreed to employ Sam at all. Perhaps they reasoned that they could get more than their money's worth out of his strong back and arms. What they didn't notice, apparently, was that Sam had a brain, too, and that he was slowly learning everything he could about the barber-and-beauty-supplies business.

Sam was living in yet another *landsleit* rooming house, owned by the Eisenberg family, in Chelsea, a scruffy, primarily Jewish section of North Boston, just across the harbor. A popular ditty of those days described the status of Chelsea. It went:

> *I wouldn't live in Chelsea*
> *And I'll tell you the reason why:*
> *A man got hit by a bag of . . . peanuts,*
> *And that's the reason why.*

Another Russian-immigrant lad also boarded with the Eisenbergs, and the two young bloods were ripe prey for Mrs. Eisenberg, who had three ripe daughters. The landlady offered her two boarders Lucullan feasts, allegedly prepared by one daughter or another, but such attentions, while appreciated, were for naught. Marriage was not immediately in Sam's plans. He was learning the beauty trade, saving his pennies, and devoutly worshipping his God in the small Chelsea Orthodox synagogues, which proliferated like those on the lower East Side. (Many of those saved pennies were sent to his sister Khaye, in Beresdiv, who saved them herself until she had enough money to leave for America, in 1913. She settled in Brooklyn, where she worked in a bridal shop, and she was known thereafter as Clara.) By 1913, Sam had his "first papers" for becoming a naturalized American citizen. By 1915, he was a bona-fide citizen—a momentous accomplishment for any immigrant—and he had been promoted by his bosses to hair mixer: the person who selects, treats, and combs over upright steel spikes the hair for a particular wig or switch. By 1916, he had a sizable nest egg put aside and a revived interest in Hasidism. He thought once again of becoming a scholar-rabbi—or, at least, a teacher—but the pull of the mercantile world was stronger. He was twenty-four years old in 1916, an American on his way up, and it occurred to him that he had no wife to stand by him. He liked the Eisenberg daughters, but not well enough to marry one of them. Still, a man of his ambition needed a good wife.

Sam's fellow-boarder had often spoken about some distant cousins who lived in the Merrimack River mill town of Lawrence, about twenty-five miles north of Boston. They were a large family called Resnick, and the oldest daughter was comely. One fall Sunday in 1916, he talked Sam into accompanying him on the long trolley ride to Lawrence.

*T*HE CROSSROADS CITY OF Shepetovka, a day's walk south from the village of Beresdiv, was prospering in 1893. It sat beside a new railway line, and river traffic on the Goryn called at its piers. There were industries and busy markets, and while most of the houses in the city were cramped and crude a few were sprawling estates, with iron gates and fine lawns and servants' quarters. The wealthier Shepetovkans were landlords and factory owners, who did not encourage Jews within the Pale to work for them but didn't discourage them, either. The Jewish population of Shepetovka was comparatively large but it was confined to an inner-city ghetto.

Simcha Resnick and his recent bride, the former Perel Zorfas, arrived in Shepetovka in 1893, he to work in a fur-processing factory and she to raise children and help out with the family finances in any way she could. They both came from the Ukrainian town of Sudilkov; their forebears were ordinary people, neither scholars nor rabbis nor legendary blacksmiths. The most memorable ancestor was Perel's father, Eliezer Zorfas, who was a charming teller of stories, which he collected through his work as a travelling metalsmith within the Pale. What Perel and Simcha perhaps lacked in distinguished family background they made up for in their zest for the present. Perel was a handsome woman, though chunky and slightly taller than Simcha, whose face was kindly and intelligent. They both liked tasty food, music, dancing, and the company of friends. No Hasids by any means, they were nevertheless religious. They were also desperately poor.

The newlyweds rented two shabby rooms in a house owned by a widow and her sons. While Simcha worked in the factory, Perel, the more enterprising of the two, started a tiny business by buying dairy products from farmers and selling them to her neighbors. She continued this basic commerce throughout her pregnancies. The first child died in infancy from the plague. The second, a girl born on the first day of spring in 1898, was luckier and healthier. They named her Charna, after Eliezer Zorfas's wife, who had died just the year before. Two more babies followed in rapid succession: Malka Leah, in late 1899, and Yosef, in 1902. It wasn't long before Charna, young as she was, became a surrogate mother to her siblings, especially after Simcha and his brother, David, went off together to America in 1903 and Perel remained in Shepetovka as the sole support of the family. (For a father to leave his family behind while he emigrated to a better life was not uncommon then, the understanding being that he would soon be able to send enough money for his wife and children to join him. However, things didn't always work out that way.)

Although her mother warned her to stay away from the Gentiles' streets of Shepetovka, Charna liked to wander, sometimes with her little sister and brother in tow. Once, entranced by strolling street musicians, she toddled after them through the city to a park. She became lost and, exhausted, finally fell asleep on the grass. The next thing she knew, she was rudely collared by a czarist policeman, who dragged her home to a frantic Perel. The ensuing spanking didn't stop her wanderlust. She continued to follow musicians or go swimming in the Goryn or stray into the busy marketplace, cadging sweets from vendors—dangerous habits for a Jewish child.

She was a bright and imaginative girl—so bright, in fact, that Perel hired one of her landlady's sons, a *malamud*, to tutor her in Russian and Hebrew. That was not ordinarily done for a daughter. Soon, the tutoring became financially impossible, but Charna hid in the *malamud's* room and listened to the other students learn. When her sister was sick with diphtheria, Charna was sent to live for a while with relatives in Sudilkov. She was spared from the diphtheria, but was later afflicted with what was generally called "consumption," probably tuberculosis. She was coughing blood. A Russian doctor was consulted, and he said that Charna should eat black bread with slabs of lard as a sure remedy. If the prescription had been black bread covered with arsenic trichloride, it couldn't have had a more horrifying effect on her meticulously kosher mother. But the doctor insisted that if the girl was to survive she must eat large portions of rendered hog fat. So Perel went to the Gentile butcher and bought lard. (I like to think she went in disguise and with an ancient Hebrew prayer of contrition on her lips.) She smeared the lard on black bread, coated it all with coarse salt (maybe that would somehow kosher it), and, when she was positive that nobody was watching, stuffed her oldest child with the strange, forbidden medicine. Amazingly, the medicine—or something—worked. In the fall of 1905, Charna was well enough to leave for America with her mother, sister, brother, and a cousin named Haskel. For almost three years, Simcha had been working as a wool-handler in the textile mills of Lawrence, Massachusetts. From the five dollars a week he earned, he had saved enough money for their steerage berths and sponsorship.

The voyage from Riga (there was no need to steal across the border, since no draft-age males were in the Resnick family) was a three-week nightmare. First, cousin Haskel was prevented from accompanying them on the ship, because he was too distant a relative, but tough and resourceful Perel convinced the authorities that Haskel was really her son. The trip continued as planned, with a new "son" named Haskel Resnick. Once on the open sea, they all wished that they had been turned back to Shepetovka. The waves were quaking mountains, and some people in steerage were dying. There seemed to be no end to the torture. Substantial food was out of the question. The days and nights of wailing filled Charna's mind—especially her mother's continuous Yiddish incantation that they "overcome the sea, please let us overcome the sea." Then, to complete the nightmare, a cargo barrel broke loose and struck Charna's arm, breaking her wrist. All that her mother could do was bandage the wrist tightly and pray that New York City indeed existed somewhere. One day, the city skyline appeared like a row of fairy-tale castles, and they were herded ashore onto Ellis Island. The bleak, echoing halls, crammed with the frightened and the sick, were at least terra firma.

Hungry, her arm aching, a red tam covering her pigtails, her feet wobbling in outsized overshoes, Charna was at last able to swallow real food and sleep on a still surface. A doctor treated her wrist, and a man in a blue uniform gave her a new name—Jennie, his version of Charna. (Perel was renamed Pearl, Malka Leah became Elizabeth, and Yosef, of course, Joseph.) For Jennie, Ellis Island started to be an adventure. But Simcha wasn't there to meet them, and they were consequently detained for two days. What Jennie has recalled most vividly of those two days was her mother's rescuing a small boy from the immigrant's ultimate horror —deportation. The boy had travelled alone, and the examining officials on Ellis Island discovered that he was infested with lice. They assigned the sorry child to the deportation area, but Pearl managed to get hold of him and some naphtha soap first. She dragged the lad into a shower room, stripped him bare, and proceeded to scrub his body and his clothes until every louse had been naphthalized to death. The officials called out his name for deportation before his clothes were dry. Pearl quickly dressed him in his sopping togs and sent him to the lineup, where he was declared wet but liceless. He passed inspection and was permitted to enter America. "She performed a miracle," Jennie has said about the incident. (The boy grew up to become a successful insurance broker in Boston. After decades of fruitless tracing, he finally learned the whereabouts of Pearl Resnick in 1935, but, alas, she had just died. He promised the family that he would sit *shivah*—a seven-day mourning period of abstinence and prayer—for Pearl, just as if he had been her son.)

Forty-eight hours later, when the adventure of the New World was wearing a little thin for Jennie, Simcha turned up to sponsor his family and gain their release. He, too, had been renamed by those capricious Ellis Island christeners—he was Samuel, for some reason—but they were all still Resnicks, a reunited family. They hugged and kissed one another, and then they boarded a ferry to Manhattan and the railroad station. The train ride to Lawrence took the rest of the day and much of the night.

Samuel Resnick was still a new immigrant himself, who could scarcely speak English, but he provided fairly well for his arriving family. Although he had started working as a common wool-handler at the gargantuan red brick mills of the American Woolen Company, along the Merrimack River, his experience in the Shepetovka fur-processing factory helped him advance to the position of weaver, which paid a bit more than the usual five-dollar-a-week immigrant's salary. Remembering the ingredients for a positive-black fur dye he had used in Russia, he experimented in Lawrence until he reproduced the formula. He travelled to Boston to try to interest some furriers in his dye. The furriers told him that nothing would come of it; then they proceeded to patent the chemical, stealing it outright. Later, Samuel found out about the theft, but, still the fearful greenhorn, he kept his anger to himself. A new immigrant did not bring legal action against established Boston merchants if he knew what was good for him.

The place Samuel rented for his family was a five-room apartment in an old frame house on Oak Street, in the heart of a crowded neighborhood populated by Italian, Polish, Syrian, Armenian, Irish, and Jewish millworkers. Jennie has recalled it as "another Ellis Island," especially the Resnick apartment, which was a kind of way station for newly arrived cousins and friends. "Sometimes I'd wake up in the middle of the night and find a relative I had never seen before sleeping in my bed," Jennie has said. "It was always open house for everybody on Oak Street." Besides Samuel, Pearl, Jennie, Elizabeth (soon called Betty), Joseph, Samuel's brother David, and the itinerant immigrants, an infant son, Louis (named, vaguely, after the deceased grandfather Eliezer) joined the family roughly nine months after the parents' reunion. (Haskel, the adopted son, had gone to live with closer relatives, in Chelsea.) "We were poor, but we never knew it," Jennie has said. "My mother was a wonderful cook, with always good things to eat on the table, no matter how broke we were. The people in the neighborhood got along, despite their different backgrounds, and everyone was nice to everyone else. Maybe the Irish weren't so friendly, but the Syrians would invite us to their weddings and whatnot, and I remember them sitting in a circle and clapping their hands all together. It was very exciting. And smack in the middle of every neighborhood activity was my mother. If somebody needed shoes fixed, she got the shoes fixed. When an Irish kid had the croup and almost choked on his own phlegm, she stuck her finger down his throat and got the phlegm out. She was the Good Samaritan. But we all helped each other. Who else would help us? There was no such thing as welfare."

For a while, Jennie had a childhood. She had to assist Pearl with the household chores and be a second mother for the younger children, but she also found new friends her own age to play with and to learn English from. The Resnicks' best friends were a family named Jacobs. One of the Jacobs daughters taught school in Lawrence, and she encouraged the Resnicks to educate Jennie. However, Miss Jacobs, mindful of their financial circumstances, advised them to register Jennie at City Hall and at the local grammar school as being two years older than she actually was, so that she could start working in the mills when she was only twelve. On record, she would appear to be fourteen, the minimum age for child labor then. That was the accepted ruse among the poor of Lawrence.

Because Jennie could read and write, albeit Russian and Hebrew, and because she quickly learned English from the street, as it were, she was placed in the fourth grade of a Lawrence elementary school when she was eight years old. She was promoted to the fifth grade, at the intermediate

Sam and Jennie

Tarbox School, where two teachers—a Miss English and a Miss Lawlor—were impressed by her. Jennie, in turn, was so impressed by them that she decided to become a teacher herself and attend normal school after high school. For four years, she held on to that dream, studying whenever her chores allowed her some free moments. But by the time she was thirteen there were two more Resnick daughters—Bertha and Dorothy—and with a household consisting of six children, a father who made ten dollars a week, a mother who had her hands full, and a lingering parade of destitute immigrant relatives, Jennie, the oldest child, was compelled to go to work. The textile mills were hiring fourteen-year-olds, and Jennie, according to the records, was fifteen. She left school and began to work as a weaver's helper at the Arlington Mills, in Lawrence. Her childhood had abruptly ended.

She awakened at 5 A.M. every working day and helped her mother wash diapers and cook breakfast and feed the babies. Starting time at the mill was 6:30 A.M.; from that hour until 5 P.M., she wheeled wagons full of large thread spools to the weavers at their looms. "The sound of those machines going all day long was earsplitting," Jennie has said. "And you could hardly breathe for the dust in the air. It was freezing cold in the winter, and in the summer it was boiling hot. Most of the windows didn't even open. I remember how once, during a lunch break, I tried to open a window so I could see outside. I couldn't budge it. So with my fingernail I scraped the dirt from the window pane and looked out. I saw down below on a little bit of grass the Yankee owners and managers of the mill playing golf—practicing their putting or whatever—during *their* lunch break. Did that make me mad! There they were, the rich men, the bosses, playing golf while the rest of us—just kids, some of us—were slaving in the heat and the noise and the dirt, our fingers bleeding all over the place. And such terrible accidents, too! Later on, I used to read dime novels about those blue bloods, which we called them, and their lives sounded so glamorous I wanted to be like them, to better myself. I even imagined that some day I'd be hob-nobbing with them. The bitterness finally just went away." At the end of every working week, Jennie brought home eight dollars, which she handed directly to Pearl. With sol-emn ritual, Pearl handed her back fifty cents. "That fifty cents used to make me so happy—I can't tell you," Jennie has said. "It was just for me, to spend any way I wanted. I knew I was helping the family live better. It never occurred to me that I should deserve more than the fifty cents."

With the Resnicks' income nearly doubled, Pearl, who had developed an eye for real estate, bought a small house on Pine Street, in a thickly settled Syrian-Armenian dis-trict. What most attracted Pearl to the house was that its ground-floor front could be used as a variety store, a poten-tial source of more income through the sale of newspapers, magazines, groceries, and candy. She opened her store and enjoyed a modest success, especially selling ethnic foods. Her youngest child, Dorothy, was an infant, but the others were pretty much able to take care of themselves; indeed, Betty would soon be old enough to work in the mills, too, and Joseph already had a newspaper route. At first, the children were fascinated by their Middle Eastern neigh-bors' customs—the mashing of fish with almonds and herbs, the strange Levantine rites of life and death—but later the Syrians were somehow confused with the gypsies around Lawrence, and the fascination turned to trepida-tion. "Watch out or the gypsies will steal you!" became the parental threat—one that was carried over into my gener-ation, by the way. My mother said later, "I began to feel funny about the Syrians, and that was long before Israel. I also had a bad incident with a Syrian girl."

Jennie managed to find time to go to night school—a special three-night-a-week institution for young millworkers—and she relished studying English literature, French and civics. Perhaps, she thought, she could still become a teacher. At one point, she left the mill to work in a Lawrence department store, at the women's neckwear counter, in order to allow more hours for her schooling, but the pay simply wasn't good enough. She returned to the Arlington Mills just in time for the notorious Lawrence textile workers' strike of 1912.

The strike came about because of a Massachusetts law requiring mill hands to work no more than fifty-four hours a week instead of fifty-six. The Boston owners responded by docking each employee twenty cents a week (the minimum wage was ten cents an hour), and thousands of American Woolen Company workers—among them Samuel Resnick—walked out. Soon, the strike spread through the nine major mills of Lawrence, as twenty-seven thousand workers, representing a wide variety of nationalities and persuasions, were stirred to daring militancy by leaders of the Industrial Workers of the World, such as Big Bill Haywood and Elizabeth Gurley Flynn. To the old-line "Americans," the strike was an outrage, and they overreacted. The police and state militiamen were called out. For nine weeks, they battled the strikers, including women and children, and committed brutalities that shocked the nation. Everyone got into the act—radicals, politicians, clergymen, celebrities, anarchists—and soup kitchens, rallying areas, and first-aid stations sprouted throughout the city. The poet James Oppenheim was moved to write of the bloody struggle: "Hearts starve as well as bodies; give us bread but give us roses!" The immigrant strikers were both pitied as victims and deplored as thankless foreigners, but in the end they proved that they could be organized into a new force for social justice—that they were no longer just a passive labor pool. They won a ten-per-cent raise, an increase in overtime pay, and some fringe benefits; more significantly, they awakened labor's consciousness across the nation. Capitalists never again viewed immigrant workers in quite the same light. That was the "roses."

The strike of 1912 had a devastating effect on the Resnicks. At the outset, Samuel left his job at the American Woolen Company, Jennie was out of work at the Arlington Mills, and Betty never got a chance to start toiling at the Wood Worsted Mill. The crucial issue for the Resnicks wasn't social justice; it was, simply, how to put bread on the table for the large family. Pearl's tiny variety store emerged as the sole support for the family, but during the labor troubles not many people in the neighborhood had much money to spend in variety stores. The Resnick sympathy was, of course, with the strikers, but that was as far as it went—just sympathy. No marching against the militia, no picketing outside plant gates, no carrying banners reading "WE WANT BREAD AND ROSES TOO." When things seemed truly desperate, Jennie heard that there were openings at the General Electric factory in Lynn, twenty miles to the southeast. Arrangements were made for her to stay with family friends there, and off she went to Lynn to make light bulbs. When I once asked her how she felt about working in Lynn while her former co-workers were on strike, she just shrugged. "I had to be a provider," she said. (During the Boston Police Strike of 1919, her brother Joseph was a full-fledged scab, hiring himself out to the city as an impromptu cop—probably with a shrug.)

After the strike, Jennie returned to her mill job in Lawrence. The pay was somewhat better and the workers had earned a new respect from the bosses, although acrimony was still in the air along with the fabric dust. Just as her childhood was iffy, so was her adolescence. She continued her strenuous routine as a weaver's helper, surrogate mother, and night-school student, hardly noticing that she was turning into an attractive woman, with flashing brown eyes, classic features ("like an Italian movie star," her sister

Bertha once said), and a full, womanly body, unfortunately supported by those heavy "Resnick" feet. Her physical development, however, did not escape the notice of a Mr. White, supervisor at the Arlington Mills, who promoted Jennie to a clerical job at ten dollars a week—the same salary as her father was making. "Mr. White took a shine to me," Jennie has recalled. "He said he'd teach me bookkeeping, how to copy invoices—that sort of thing. He used to pet me this way and that—never too far, because he knew I wouldn't allow it. I was so naïve. I didn't know anything. Nobody told me anything. And he was a married man, too! Most of the girls in the office were Americans, not immigrants. The ones I used to work with became jealous; they shied away from me. 'What's the big idea?' they wanted to know. One of them, a Syrian girl, was really nasty jealous. She slapped me and called me a 'dirty Jew.' I never forgave her for that. And I never again liked Syrians so much." Jennie was fifteen—seventeen on her record.

Perhaps Mr. White's advances stirred a sense of her own womanliness. Before long, she started going to dances on weekends, even to Canobie Lake—a forbidden spot, with a real band and a wide variety of patrons. She had a crush on a young Gentile mill foreman, and one night he asked her to dance with him. "I was so thrilled," Jennie has said. "Of course, my mother never knew. I managed to keep some things from her. You see, I wasn't thinking of myself as an immigrant anymore. I was a regular American."

It may well have been that Jennie had managed to keep some things from her mother, but Pearl knew a marriageable daughter when she saw one. The way out of poverty for a nice Jewish girl was to marry a nice Jewish man, who would provide for her. Thus it was in the Old Country; thus it would be in America. With this principle firmly in mind, Pearl announced in the fall of 1916 (when Jennie was eighteen) that a Chelsea cousin and his friend, Samuel Joseph Bernstein, were coming to Lawrence to spend Sunday with the Resnicks. Pearl prepared a feast for the visitors, and a rather stilted first meeting took place between Sam and Jennie. "The two of them walked into our house on Pine Street, and I could tell right away that they both smack-dab fell for me," Jennie has recalled. "They looked like a couple of greenhorns. My cousin was handsomer and taller than Sam, but Sam wasn't so bad-looking, either. He still had curly hair, but he wore glasses. Right away, I didn't like his glasses or his accent, and I didn't like his suit, because it had no belt in the back. Also, he wasn't wearing pointed shoes, which were the big fashion then, like the belted suit jacket. My best chum was there—Doris Smith, a beautiful blond Jewish girl who was from England—and the two of us just sat and giggled every time Sam talked. Finally, it got so bad that Doris and I left to go out to Canobie Lake, and the two fellows sat there with my mother and father. That was that."

But it wasn't. With Pearl's encouragement, the cousin and Sam made regular trips to Lawrence. In fact, they were invited to come on Saturday night and stay until Sunday night. Jennie continued to ignore them, heading for Canobie Lake whenever she could, but her parents were enthralled—especially with Sam, whom they found to be intelligent, ambitious, and blessed with a notable family in the Old Country. (The fame of the Bernsteins of Beresdiv was known even unto the Resnicks of Shepetovka.) Sam never failed to bring little gifts for the family—Jennie was in the habit of spurning *her* little gift—and he flattered Pearl on her cooking and housekeeping. With his namesake and potential father-in-law, he would sit for hours and discuss the Bible, philosophy, and current events. They were both devotees of the Yiddish press. The chillier Jennie was toward Sam, the warmer were her parents.

After several months of this fruitless routine, the cousin and Sam each asked Pearl for Jennie's hand, without either knowing of the other's action. Pearl counselled them, separately, to have patience. Sam was the more tenaciously patient; the cousin dropped out of the marital sweepstakes after a few more weeks. Meanwhile, Pearl worked on her oldest daughter. "You'll be an old maid till your hair is gray," she told Jennie. "You're missing your chance. Sam's a good man with a good job. He's going places." Slowly, Pearl's browbeating had its effect. What helped to sweeten Sam's image in Jennie's eyes was his sense of humor. "He always had a good story to tell, and he always knew a joke," Jennie has said. "He made me laugh. There was that and the fact he was so persistent." At one point, she was even a bit jealous. Sam had invited the entire Resnick clan to his digs in Chelsea for an afternoon's visit. Mrs. Eisenberg, his landlady, presented a heavy table for the visitors and made sure that her three daughters were looking their best. In a loud aside to Sam during the meal, Mrs. Eisenberg commented that Jennie was "so thin she could be a consumptive." That overheard observation and Sam's obvious friendliness with the well-fed Eisenberg daughters distressed Jennie. She later asked Sam, with mock disinterest, "Why don't you marry one of them, they're all nice-looking girls?" Sam answered—for the first time directly to Jennie —that he wanted to marry only one girl in the whole world, and her name was Jennie Resnick.

Still, Jennie wasn't prepared to say yes outright. It took a devilish ruse conceived by Pearl to make the engagement official. Sam had bought a modest engagement ring, which he gave to Pearl. Pearl, in turn, instructed Betty, who shared a bedroom with Jennie, to slip the ring on Jennie's finger while she slept. Jennie awakened the next morning with the surprise of her life: she was engaged and there was a real diamond ring on her finger to prove it. "To this day, I don't like surprises," Jennie has told me. "But I took Sam seriously after that. I figured he really wanted to marry me. Mother made an engagement party, and a wedding date was set before I even knew what was happening. I still went out dancing, though. Sam didn't like dancing. He had two left feet."

One large obstacle blocked their path to the altar. The First World War—which up to then had occasioned only snarls and curses whenever the Kaiser's name was mentioned—became a real threat when the United States entered the hostilities, in the spring of 1917. Just after Sam's engagement was announced that summer, he, like so many other young men, was drafted. He was given a patriotic leave of absence from Frankel & Smith, and, by chance, he was inducted in Lawrence and assigned for his basic training to Camp Devens, in Ayer, Massachusetts, only thirty miles to the southwest. As the motley inductees marched down Essex Street in Lawrence to the train station for the short ride to Camp Devens, Jennie and her family screamed and cried when they spotted Sam stumbling along with the others. "I thought he was going off to war and I would never see him again," Jennie has said. "That's when I broke down." The first real element of romance had entered into their relationship.

But Sam was not cut out to be a soldier, either in the czar's army or in Woodrow Wilson's. With commendable candor, he once told me how inept he was at close-order drill in the tent city that was Camp Devens. "I couldn't get the instructions straight," he said. "The sergeant would yell something, and everyone would know what he was saying except me. When it rained, the whole place turned into a pigsty and the tents fell down. Everything was outdoors. You shaved with cold water, you showered with cold water. I never had enough time to do anything right." (Almost forty years later, I spent the last few months of my two-year Army hitch at the same post. It was then called Fort Devens, and except that wooden barracks had replaced the tents things hadn't changed much.) The great moment of revelation for both Sam and the Army came on his first visit to the rifle range. Not even his new government-issue eyeglasses could correct his severe lifelong myopia. He was handed a Springfield rifle and was told to shoot at a target. He missed so alarmingly that he was relieved of further range duty. A more thorough eye examination by Army doctors followed, and before long he was relieved of all military duty. One Saturday night in the early fall of 1917, he returned unannounced to Lawrence and walked into the kitchen of the new Resnick house, on Juniper Street. Jennie squealed with joy and then impulsively hugged and kissed him, in front of the entire family. He was an honorably discharged veteran.

*T*HE ONLY RELIABLE NEWS OF the family Sam had left behind in Russia was from his sister Clara, who had settled in Brooklyn in 1913. Since the onset of the war, in 1914, letters did not get through. The family's situation, up to the time of Clara's flight to America, had been fluid. Frustration with the czar's erratic autocracy had infected most classes and cultures, including the *shtetl* Jews, although Yudel and Dinah Bernstein had maintained their old ways and kept out of politics. If anything, sociopolitical events made Yudel and Dinah all the more determined to preserve their traditional life. Of their four surviving children, the two older ones had deserted them and fled to America. But even worse, their younger son, Shlomo, was attracted to the godless Socialist revolutionaries. Only their younger daughter, Sura-Rivka, was more or less stable and faithful. In 1920, she met and married a good Jewish man named Srulik Zvainboim from the then Polish town of Mezhiritsh, about twenty miles from Beres-

div. The young couple moved across the border to Mezhiritsh and raised a good Jewish family of four sons—Mikhoel,
born in 1921; Meir, born in 1924; Bezalel (another namesake of the legendary blacksmith), born in 1928; and Men-
del, born in 1933—but their circumstances were harsh.
Srulik, the burdened father and husband, had no trade and
provided for his family by performing odd jobs and occasionally receiving financial help from American relatives,
especially my father.

Several years passed before Sam was to learn much more
about his brother, Shlomo. Since he was only twelve years
old, Shlomo was too young to fight in the 1917 revolution,
although his sympathies were with the Bolsheviks. He had
continued to live restlessly with Yudel and Dinah in Beresdiv until 1922, when he illegally crossed the Polish border
to visit Sura-Rivka in Mezhiritsh, but he was depressed by
what he saw there and returned to Russia determined to
improve himself by studying for a profession. Changing his
first name to the more Russian-sounding "Semyon," he
attended a worker's institute, toiled as a coal miner in the
Donets Basin, and was finally graduated from a mining-
engineering school in Dnepropetrovsk, the Ukraine. As an
engineer at the coal fields near Moscow, he began a steady
climb up the Party ladder—one of the young technocrats.
During that climb, he married a Jewish Communist named
Fanye, from his hometown of Beresdiv, and they lived together with their infant son, Aleksandr, in a tiny Moscow
apartment. Shlomo, who in 1908 had tearfully begged his
older brother to take him along to America, had chosen
another escape route from the ghetto to independence.
The two brothers had thrown in their lots with the two
major opposing forces of the twentieth century—American
capitalism and Russian Communism. In a sense, it was like
those Civil War stories of two brothers—one in gray, the
other in blue—facing each other on the field at Gettys-
burg.

Sam and Jennie

*T*HE DATE SET FOR THE BERN-
stein-Resnick nuptials was Sunday, October 28, 1917. The
plan was to have the ceremony take place at a small Lawrence synagogue, complete with *chuppa* (marriage canopy)
and bearded Orthodox rabbi, and then the dozens of relatives and friends would remove to the Resnick house, on
Juniper Street, where one of Pearl's finest feasts would be
laid out. The new house was an indication of better times
for the family. Even though Jennie had quit her job just
before the wedding, there were three other mill salaries
coming in—from the father, Betty, and Joseph. And financially auspicious was Pearl's entry into the real-estate business with the help of a Mr. Kussel; her first transaction was
to sell her house and variety store on Pine Street and, with
the profit, buy the larger Juniper Street house. The Resnicks were by no means well off, but they could comfortably treat their first daughter to a grand wedding, with an
abundance of good things to eat, professional musicians to
play, and plenty of guests to enjoy it all.

Pearl's preparations began weeks in advance. She bought
the wedding dress for Jennie, but she sewed the bridesmaid
dresses, of pale-green voile, for her other daughters. Gallons of wine and a cordial called *parilla* (consisting of fer-
mented dates, prunes, and figs) were manufactured in the
cellar, and Pearl baked at her coal-fired oven day and night.
She loved to cook. Her daughters remembered her passing
the long hours at the stove by singing—one hand on her
sizable hip, the other stirring a pot—everything from sentimental Yiddish ballads to snatches of operatic arias she
had picked up. She hired two Polish women and a man to
clean and boil scores of chickens in huge copper kettles,
and when all the food was finally ready on the day before

the wedding she declared the living room off limits to everybody, covered the tables with white sheets, and laid out the banquet. Her last words of advice to Jennie, a few minutes before they left for the *shul*, harked back to Russian-Jewish folklore: "When the rabbi speaks, step on Sam's foot and you will always be the boss." Her daughter did as she was told. Decades later, Jennie said ruefully, "How wrong could my mother be!"

After the ceremony, a milling crowd of invited guests and inquisitive neighborhood people gathered outside the house on Juniper Street. The excitement prompted a reporter-photographer from the Lawrence *Eagle-Tribune* to crash the party by climbing in through a bedroom window. Unfortunately, he was rebuffed by Jennie's brothers, so there is no graphic record of the event. But from the testimony of everybody who was there it was a roaring celebration. The bride and groom, appropriately nervous at the start, relaxed during the endless toasts to their health and happiness. Especially Sam. He liked to knock back his schnapps in the Russian-peasant manner—a small, neat glassful down the hatch, no chaser—and he soon was attempting the *kazatsky* and the transported choreography of the Hasid. (He may have had two left feet when it came to conventional dancing, as Jennie has said, but given a little schnapps and some encouragement from one of those reedy bands at a wedding or a bar mitzvah, he was off— usually, as I recall, to the accompaniment of my mother's whispered "Sam, remember your ulcer.")

Late that night, the bloated, exhausted guests departed —except for some out-of-town relatives who were staying on at the Resnick house. Strangely, no arrangements for the marriage's consummation had been planned for that evening. The signal event would presumably be effected when the newlyweds honeymooned at a Boston hotel the following day. Jennie—a girlish nineteen, untutored, frightened—was just as happy to be assigned to her old bedroom, which that night she shared with her sister Betty and a visiting female cousin. Sam—perhaps less naïve and certainly more amorous—was given a bed in the room of Jennie's brothers, Joseph and Louis. Brother Joe, an independent fifteen-year-old and something of a practical joker, slyly informed his anxious new brother-in-law that Jennie would slip into the bedroom in the middle of the night and the two would be left alone. At the appointed hour, a dark figure stole into Sam's bed. The dark figure was Joe, not Jennie. Sam never quite forgave Joe for that prank.

The real honeymoon night was not much better, and surely less jocular. Sam had booked a room in the Essex Hotel, near South Station in downtown Boston. For him, it was the height of available luxury and romance. However, the noise of the steam locomotives kept them both on edge. The next day, they moved into a rented room in Mattapan (he had judiciously given up his space at the Eisenberg ménage in Chelsea), and the marriage was at last consummated. The day after that, Sam returned to his labors of mixing and weaving human hair at Frankel & Smith. Jennie cooked and cared for Sam, cleaned their flat, and learned the role of a proper housewife in Mattapan, then a predominantly Jewish working-class section of Boston. By the end of November, she was pregnant and had a lot to discuss with the other housewives in the neighborhood. Meanwhile, Sam's new stability and his rededication to duty had so impressed his employers that they appointed him assistant manager, at a salary of fifteen dollars a week. He may still have had the hayseed of Beresdiv in his hair, but there was no denying his worth to the firm. "Sam was working like a slave day and night," Jennie has said, "and I was getting big with the baby. It wasn't the way I imagined it from the books I read."

Before long, sharp differences emerged between them— differences in their personalities and goals, mainly. Since romance had not been a large element in their marriage, similar ambitions and mutual respect were essential to hold them together. But ambitions and respect were precisely the problems from the first. In the broadest sense, it was the old Apollonian-Dionysian conflict. Sam was the driven, diligent Horatio Alger hero, willing to slave and sacrifice in order to better his lot. Also, he was an intellectual, albeit a parochial one, the descendant of noted rabbinical scholars; his avocational pursuits were solely concerned with the mind—Talmudic study, philosophical discussion, the science of business. The uses of the mind, education of any sort, were paramount to him. On paper, at least, Jennie was more "educated" than Sam. She had, after all, gone to night school and had studied a variety of academic subjects, while Sam's formal education had never progressed beyond a few years at a *shtetl* yeshiva. Her schooling had been rudely curtailed by work in the mills, however, and her early marriage and impending motherhood had further turned her away from cerebral matters. Her chief interests seemed to be food, the small available pleasures of life in Mattapan, movies and their celluloid celebrities, romantic novels, the local Hearst newspaper, and gossip with her coevals. None of these things—with the occasional exception of food—held the slightest interest for her husband.

Increasingly, he grew contemptuous of what he saw as her dullness, her passive acceptance of the superficial, the second-rate. He contrived to blame the Resnicks for her condition. She was following the "Resnick" way of life— common and earthy—that was her fate, her curse. His earlier respect and affection for Pearl and Samuel Resnick abruptly vanished. (Throughout their years together, domestic arguments inevitably ended with Sam calling Jennie "you Resnick, you," which in his vernacular was tantamount to saying, "You are dumb and ordinary." By implication, everything "Bernstein" was bright and exceptional. Needless to say, Sam's relations with the Resnick family deteriorated after his wedding day.) Jennie, while incapable of being contemptuous, made light of Sam's consuming ambition, his penny-pinching, his Talmudic studies, his visits to "those rabbis." She was not quite out of her teens, but she felt stunted. She wanted to live, to dance, to experience things, but she was trapped in confining wifehood with a man who no longer made her laugh.

It was soon clear to both of them that their marriage had been a mistake, a mismating. In that time and circumstance, divorce was out of the question—a notion entertained only in mad dreams. You stuck it out, especially with a baby on the way, no matter what, for better for worse. Typically, Sam was hard at work in Boston when the baby was due. Jennie had gone alone to Lawrence toward the end of August, 1918, to be with her family and to lie in at the Lawrence General Hospital. At 3 A.M. on Sunday, August 25th, she went into labor. Dr. Meyer Schwartz, the Resnick family physician and neighborhood character, was notified, and he appeared with his trademarks—a crushed porkpie hat on his head and a well-chewed stogie in his mouth. He took Jennie and her parents to the hospital, where, shortly, a scrawny son was born. At Pearl's insistence, he was named Louis—like Jennie's brother, after Eliezer Zorfas, the father of Pearl. With a twelve-year-old uncle and his infant nephew both named Louis in the same household, confusion reigned, so the infant was called Leonard, which was Jennie and Sam's preference all along. (Until the age of sixteen, he was known by his legal name of Louis to his teachers in school, while everybody else called him Leonard. At sixteen, he legally changed his name at the Lawrence City Hall.)

After Lenny's birth, the marriage improved somewhat. Samuel Joseph Bernstein had a son and heir, a creature in his own image who would be possessed of a godly spirit, as all Bernstein males before him had been. He would be rigorously educated, be given every possible advantage, and would follow in whatever path to success his father was hacking through the scrubland of American commerce. Sam redoubled his efforts and ambition. Every extra hour of work was performed with his son's future in mind. And Jennie, still in Lawrence, had a new reason for living. Her son was the sole object of her love. Motherhood was her true calling. It occupied her every moment, especially since the boy was sickly from the start—asthmatic and occasionally convulsionary. ("A weak chest, like his father" Jennie often said of him.) The Resnicks adored their first grandchild, and Jennie was proud. She remembered Pearl calming the wheezing, colicky baby in a big maple rocking chair for hours on end while the rest of the family tiptoed about and helped with the diapers. Sam came to Lawrence whenever he could get away from the office. When the baby was deemed strong enough to travel, Sam took his wife and son back to Mattapan.

Sam's hard work and faith in the future paid off. Before his son was a year old, he was appointed manager of Frankel & Smith, and he could afford a bigger, more comfortable apartment in Allston, near Cambridge. Pennies were still pinched, but they were saved for a new reason: Sam was determined to put aside enough money so that he would be able to open his own business one day. He would continue to tolerate indignities from his bosses (even as their manager) in order to earn and learn enough to be their competition. His stinting on the family budget and his late hours at the office aroused some new resentment in Jennie, however, and in 1920 a bitter argument brought about the unthinkable: Jennie left Sam's bed and, with her son, she went home to Lawrence and mother. Sam immediately followed, demanding that she return to Allston with him, but Jennie refused. For two weeks, Sam stewed alone in the Allston apartment, each passing day thickening his conviction that "those Resnicks" were all a cabal conspiring against him. Actually, it was Pearl who convinced Jennie that she should go back to Sam. To sweeten the reconciliation, Pearl bought them a set of fine linen.

Within a year, they had moved again—this time to Revere, a seaside area just north of Chelsea—and another argument led to a second separation. Lenny's first clear memories occurred during the Revere period. Their apartment, just above a tailor shop, was in a large house owned by the Zion family. Two Zion sisters, Ruthie and Nettie, were extremely solicitous of Jennie and her son, helping them through a difficult time when the father had apparently moved out. One afternoon, though, their solicitousness flagged, and Lenny was left alone. He decided to experiment with the bathroom-basin taps. He climbed up onto the sink, carefully plugged in the stopper, and turned on both faucets. Like the Sorcerer's Apprentice, he discovered that he couldn't turn them off. The basin overflowed and the water seeped down to the tailor's shop, drenching several suits. "There was hell to pay," Lenny recalled. "It was a very traumatic experience—the panic of not being able to shut that water off. Of course, it never occurred to me to pull out the plug. I was just too young." But perhaps the hell that was paid, along with the damage bill to the tailor downstairs, brought Sam back to the fold. In any case, father and mother were reconciled, and soon the family moved again, to Courtland Road.

A lot happened while they lived in the two-family frame house, on that unpaved Mattapan street. For one thing, Jennie became pregnant again. On October 3, 1923, she gave birth to a daughter—who was named Shirley Anne, after, in a way, Anne Shirley, the heroine of the popular novel "Anne of Green Gables," which later became a film starring Jennie's favorite movie star, Anne Shirley. The birth coincided with another momentous event for the family: Sam gave his notice to Frankel & Smith and opened his own place of business at 111 Summer Street, in Boston.

Enough pennies had been pinched, enough knowledge of the hair-goods-and-beauty-supplies trade had been gleaned, and the critical moment had come at last. "It was rough going from the start, a struggle," Jennie has recalled. "He had this little place on Summer Street, with just a few people working for him. There were more downs than ups, but then some of the customers of Frankel & Smith who liked him came over, and things looked a little better. His old bosses were mad when he left, but when they saw he was getting some of their customers they wanted him back in the worst way—at triple his salary, anything, if he would only come back. But no, not Sam. He loved to be on his own—independent and stubborn. That was the story of Sam—independent and stubborn. I had my hands full with Lenny, who was starting school and was still sickly, and with Shirley, just an infant. But Sam had *three* children. His own business was like another child."

One of those few people employed by the Samuel Bernstein Hair Company was Abraham Malamud, who as an eight-year-old boy in Korets had watched his first cousin disappear down a road one day to Rovno and America. They had corresponded over the years, Sam convincing Abe that his future lay in the New World. But when Abe was ready to leave Korets, in 1921, the American immigration rules and the Russian emigration laws were tighter. Abe was nevertheless resolved. He dodged the Soviet authorities, leaving behind six brothers and sisters, and made tracks for Warsaw and Danzig. In Danzig, he was told that the best route to America was via Cuba, where, after a year's residency, one could apply more expediently for immigration papers to the United States. During his year in Cuba, Abe supported himself by filling a wooden box with notions and sundries and peddling the wares on the streets of Havana with the cry, "Look in the box!" in both Spanish and English. (Those few words were just about all the Spanish and English he knew, or had to know, for several months.) With the income gained from such humble hawking, he travelled to Florida, New York City, and, finally, to his Uncle Harry Levy's house, in Hartford. There, he saw Sam—who had come to Harry's house with his wife and son—for the first time since 1908. Sam, by then the manager of Frankel & Smith, offered Abe a job as a hair-mixer. With good humor and perseverance verging on saintliness, Abe performed that task under Sam's commercial roof for more than fifty years. (My father used to say, as if he were revealing a Biblical miracle, that Abe, a devout, diminutive, gentle man with a mustache that barely concealed a slight harelip, opened and closed the office unfailingly every single business day. Then Sam would correct himself: "No, once he had a hernia operation and he missed three days in a row.") For reasons that elude everybody concerned, Sam persuaded Abe to change his last name to Miller, shortly after he took his cousin into his new business. Perhaps he thought that Malamud, meaning "teacher," was not proper for the mercantile world.

"Besides Sam, there were three of us on Summer Street," Abe Miller has recalled. "A secretary for the books and invoices, a hair-goods salesman, and me. For a long time, no money came in, so we all had to operate on a shoestring. I lived in a little room in the South End. I wasn't married to Annie yet, so I could just get by. Sam worked so hard. We all did. We believed he could make it. Then, business picked up a little when the beauty salons became popular and the women were changing their hairstyles. Pretty soon, we were doing more business in beauty-parlor supplies than in wigs and switches." Indeed, wigs and switches were doing poorly when Sam opened his office doors. Sam later wrote to an associate, "In 1923, the hair market collapsed and I was out. I discussed the situation with Mr. Tower [Russell B. Tower, Sam's "Yankee" idol and the president of the long-established Edward E. Tower Company] and he suggested that I go into the beauty-parlor-supply field and offered to help me with the necessary stock." That act of generosity by a competitor was never forgotten by Sam, who revered the sterling old New Englander. Whenever an example of gentility and integrity was called for in our family conversation, we all knew it would be Russell B. Tower.

Much of Sam's Horatio Alger climb up life's ladder was a result of good timing and good luck. The beauty-supplies business had come alive during the First World War years, when the popular dancer Irene Castle (who, with her husband, Vernon, created the one-step, the turkey trot, and the Castle Walk) bobbed her hair. Her fame was such that it became the instant rage among American women to duplicate her bob. Many men's barbershops were hurriedly converted into "beauty salons," which were outfitted by "hair companies" like Frankel & Smith (Harry Levy's barbershop in Hartford was one of the converted, and was renamed the Claire Beauty Shoppe.) The rage continued into the nineteen-twenties, with the radical flapper hairdos and the appearance of something called "the permanent wave," imported from England by a German exile named Speckermann. The permanent-wave fad was facilitated by Speckermann's invention of the Frederics Permanent Wave Machine—a monstrous device that hung from the salon ceiling, sprouting tentacles of wires leading to heating elements, which, when applied to the victim's hair with chemically treated pads, effected a more or less enduring curl. This process was sheer torture for the ladies; in some cases, it was downright perilous. However, in the mid-twenties, a new Frederics machine was designed—lighter, more tolerable, and mounted on a movable pedestal, so the salon customer didn't feel so much that she was the subject of a mad scientist's experiment—and this development meant that a beauty shop could permanently wave several clients' hair at once with comparative ease.

At first sight, Sam realized the benefits of the improved

Sam and Jennie

device and succeeded in outbidding all his Boston competition for the exclusive New England franchise. The orders for the new machines came in a torrent, some from salons hastily established just for the permanent-wave craze. "One day in 1927, I didn't have a nickel to my name," Sam used to say. "The next morning, I went into the office and it looked like every salon operator in New England wanted a Frederics. I couldn't handle all the orders with just a few people working for me, so I had to hire salesmen and secretaries and bookkeepers and shipping clerks and stockboys, all in a couple of days. I suddenly had money in the bank, credit everywhere, a name for myself—just because of Frederics. It was what you call the American Dream coming true." Indeed it was. Before long, he had rented two floors of an office building at 480 Washington Street, and since the hair goods also started to boom, he soon commanded a staff of fifty employees—including two of Jennie's sisters, Bertha and Dorothy, who worked as hair weavers.

Sam's American Dream came close to becoming a spectacular American Fantasy a few years later, when a young salesman named Charles Revson paid a call at his office. Revson represented a New Jersey cosmetics company that specialized in nail polish, but he intended to go into business for himself, bringing out durable "cream enamel" for the nails in different opaque colors. (Up to then, nail polish had been transparent and rather unstable.) He needed five hundred dollars to buy more chemicals for cooking up his concoctions on a kitchen stove. If Sam would make a five-hundred dollar investment, Revson would sign over a third of his inchoate business. What did a smart fellow, a comer like Sam Bernstein, have to say about that? Well, Sam Bernstein's face grew as red as the contents of one of Revson's bottles. When he was capable of speech, he shouted at Revson (whose name could be loosely translated as "rabbi's son"), "You're making American woman into whores!

You're painting their nails so they'll look like two-dollar whores! Get out of my office!" And so Revson left, angry and unchastened. Soon thereafter, he and a more sagacious, if less moralistic, backer named Charles Lachman founded Revlon. We Bernsteins have often amused ourselves by speculating on what our fate might have been if Sam had owned a third of the Revlon corporation. (One way or another, Revlon continued to haunt the Bernsteins. Sam's business suffered a bit in the thirties and forties because he wasn't able to acquire the profitable Revlon line of beauty supplies. Sam's moralizing changed with the times; Charles Revson's memory remained keen. Finally, though, Revson let bygones be bygones and gave Sam the Revlon line in the nineteen-fifties; actually, it was good business, since Sam's company was the biggest in New England. Then, in 1959, my sister, Shirley, who had been the producer of a television quiz show, "The $64,000 Challenge," was called to testify before a House committee on quiz show rigging. Labelled the "GIRL TV FIXER" in a *Daily News* headline and "MAESTRO'S KIN" in a *Journal-American* banner, she disclosed in an affidavit how she was forced by the show's sponsor to try to control particular contestants' abilities to answer questions correctly, depending on whether or not the sponsor liked the contestants. The sponsor of "The $64,000 Challenge" was Revlon.)

For Sam and Jennie, prosperity in the late nineteen-twenties brought with it Americanization, assimilation, upward mobility, material pleasures, grand plans. First on the agenda was moving to bigger quarters. The two children needed their own rooms; Jennie needed a better kitchen; Sam needed a quiet place for his Talmud reading and periodic brooding. The route for upwardly mobile Boston Jewish families then was from the ghettos of Chelsea or Mattapan or Dorchester to the cleaner, tree-lined streets of Roxbury, and—if the money kept coming in—to the finest prize of all, a house of one's own in Newton or

Brookline. (Back Bay, Beacon Hill, and the more stately suburbs of Wellesley Hills, Needham, Winchester, and Dedham were still the exclusive territories of the WASPs.) Even with a swelling bank account, Sam hesitated to make the giant leap to Newton or Brookline. He was no longer pinching pennies, exactly, but he didn't quite trust the economy, either. He may have been the only Republican voter in America then who didn't own a single share of stock except in the Samuel Bernstein Hair Company.

So during the next six years he moved his family to increasingly commodious apartments in Roxbury: Abbotsford Street, Crawford Street, Brookledge Street, Schuyler Street, and, finally, Pleasanton Street. The frequent transplantations nearly drove Jennie crazy—especially the one to Crawford Street. Jennie had supervised the move to the apartment and had most of the furniture in place by the time Sam arrived at his new home from the office. He was scarcely in the door when to his horror he saw a cockroach crawling up the wall. The man who had suffered through the filth of a *shtetl* farm, steerage across the Atlantic, fish-cleaning sheds, immigrant's tenements, Camp Devens, and countless other affronts to his sense of hygiene had at last had enough. He was a man of some means now, and he would not put up with a cockroach in his house. He refused to sleep even one night in that apartment. He ordered the movers to reload the furnishings. The lease was broken, and another, cleaner place was found, on Brookledge Street.

Those were intense growing-up years for the children *and* the parents. Just as Lenny and Shirley were discovering themselves as individuals, Jennie and Sam were learning new things about the glories of the good life. Jennie was allowed charge accounts at Boston department stores. Substantial furnishings were acquired, substantial enough to endure for decades in various houses: outsized beds of mahogany and maple, overstuffed sofas and chairs in

67

nappy, florid patterns, a sepia drawing of the Grand Canal, the ever-popular "Egyptian" tapestry, a genuine Oriental rug, and the inevitable red cut-glass bowl full of wax fruit. On Schuyler Street, Aunt Clara deposited her ancient upright piano, which was to have a telling effect on Lenny. Sam joined one of the older Conservative synagogues in America, Temple Mishkan Tefila, which, in 1925, had been reestablished in a white-granite Parthenon-like structure on Roxbury's Seaver Street, facing Franklin Park. His new status seemed to draw him away from the tiny, crude, sexually segregated Orthodox *shuls* of his past. Now he could take his family with pride to a place of worship the equal of any cathedral, with a choir, an organ, a reserved pew, a rabbi named H. H. Rubenovitz, who gave sermons not only in English but in Oxford-accented English, a cantor who could have been an opera singer, and a first-rate Hebrew school to further his children's sense of heritage. His children's secular education took place at the William Lloyd Garrison School, an archetypical Boston institution where development of the mind and manners was not to be trifled with. Sam, as a man of consequence in the beauty trade, attended business conventions and shows in New York and Chicago, rubbing elbows with the captains of that particular industry. And as a symbol of his true arrival he bought outright an automobile—a Ford touring car.

Like thousands of other American paterfamiliases, Sam acquired a new freedom—mobility—with his Ford. At first, he tentatively used the car on Sunday afternoons for excursions to "the country"—a term meaning anywhere just beyond the Boston city limits. When he was a little more confident behind the steering wheel, he attempted trips to Hartford, to visit Uncle Harry and Aunt Polly. The drive from Boston to Hartford in those days was a wearying one. The easiest part was down the Worcester Turnpike, or Route 9 ("the No. 9 Road," as Sam always called it; he thus prefixed every major highway, giving each road a kind of hierarchical importance). From dingy Worcester on, through the towns along "the No. 20 Road" and other such lesser routes, it was slow and tedious travelling.

Once in Hartford, however, with the warm and outgoing relatives, it was pure joy. The Levy house, on Greenfield Street, and the Kleiman (Aunt Polly's family) house, on Eastford Street, were regularly filled with people, food, music, and laughter. There were Jake and Josie and Nathalie and Nathan and Maurice Kleiman, and two Beckys ("Becky from the country" and "Becky from Meriden"), and a dozen other distant cousins and close friends. For Lenny especially, Hartford was the Nirvana of his youth. One reason was the immediate release from the tension in his own household and its replacement by fun and ease. "The Hartford folks seemed like the healthiest, least neurotic people," Lenny has said. "Uncle Harry and Aunt Polly were saints, and the others were wonderful characters. In a diary I kept when I was a kid, I made an entry about a Kleiman girl I met there, and it said at the end, 'There's no girl like Nathalie.' Josie, Nathalie's sister, sang like a bird, a sort of coloratura, and she was a musical influence on me. And, of course, there was Uncle Harry's old wind-up Victor phonograph, with records of Rosa Ponselle singing arias and Frank Munn singing 'I Want to Go Back to Michigan' and Frank Crumit singing 'I Wish That I'd Been Born in Borneo.' Hartford was an aesthetic experience. The evenings usually ended with a riotous game of penny ante at a big round dining-room table, with Aunt Polly's high-pitched shriek of laughter rising above everyone else's. I loved to lie in bed listening to all that laughter downstairs. Hartford was one of the few places where Jennie and Sam could almost relax."

On the road home to Boston, the tension would return, however—in great measure because of Sam's hair-raising driving habits. He held the steering wheel in a strangulating grip at its lowest point, his palms up and his knuckles white with the sheer effort of holding on. It seemed impossible for him to turn the wheel with that grip, but he managed to, somehow, almost always to the right. If in doubt, Sam would turn right, which tended to carry him in ever-confusing circles when he was lost in, say, Sturbridge. He drove with infuriating slowness, probably because of his poor eyesight and lack of oneness with mechanical things. The cacophony of horns behind his car was a constant embarrassment. Miraculously, he had few accidents. One of the few, on a return trip from Hartford, was potentially serious. The car skidded on wet pavement and flipped over on its side. The passengers escaped with nothing worse than cuts and slight shock. Another mishap involved only a tangling of bumpers, but it is nevertheless memorable; in fact, it is Lenny's favorite story of his youth. Sam had plowed into the rear of another Ford, locking bumpers, and both drivers got out of their cars to inspect the damage. The other driver, a towering black man, claimed that his fender had also been dented, whereupon Sam grew angry and argumentative. As their roadside debate became more heated, Sam muttered a Yiddish curse and said something disparaging about black people operating cars. The black man squared his shoulders, held his fist an inch from Sam's nose, and shouted, "You shut up, you goddam Irishman!"

*T*HE ONSET OF THE GREAT Depression and its attendant suffering contrarily brought even more prosperity to Sam and his family. Since he had owned no stock before October of 1929, he had no worthless certificates to burn thereafter. And since he was a scrupulous saver of excess funds the dollars in his account at a sound bank doubled and tripled in buying power. Most contrary of all was how the Depression affected the beauty business. One would think that the first frivolous item to be excised from any family's skimpy budget during hard times would be a visit to the beauty salon. However, many women who had, say, twenty dollars to spend would use half of it for food and the other half for a perm. It was Sam's theory that female vanity accounted for this odd fiscal behavior, along with the morale-boosting effect that sessions at the salons had on depressed ladies. Of course, some hairdressers were pinched by the economic situation, and bankruptcies were fairly common, but Sam extended credit, at no interest, to all customers whom he trusted, and he thus rescued many of them from disaster. Decades later, I would meet by chance some aging Massachusetts salon owner who would tell me something like "Oh, you're Sam Bernstein's boy. I wouldn't be in business today if it wasn't for your father. He saved my neck during the Depression." These unsolicited encomiums occurred often enough to make my father rather heroic in my eyes, as well as in the eyes of his older clients. Sam himself was ambivalent about hairdressers, though. While he joshed and flattered them, as any good jobber would, he reserved his respect for a precious few—those he thought were reasonably intelligent. "Hairdressers are ignorant women," he was wont to say, especially after a rough day at the office or at a beauty show. "They carry on like a bunch of two-dollar whores. All they think about is drinking and playing around with my salesmen. They can't hold on to a dime. They don't even read the newspaper. Stupid women!" In a way, his opinion of hairdressers formed his more general view of womanhood. Whenever some female (hairdresser or not) had crossed him, he was apt to bellow, "Woman!"—after she was out of earshot. Many of the "Woman!"s I heard from Sam were directed at my mother.

The growing Bernstein fortune, flying in the face of a smashed economy, emboldened Sam to strike out for the grand prize—a house of his own. Actually, he went one better and made plans to build *two* houses—a "winter house" on Park Avenue in suburban Newton and a "summer house" on Lake Avenue in the country town of Sharon. In 1931, when they were living in a comfortable rented house on Pleasanton Street, in Roxbury, and had the services of a full-time maid named Agnes, Sam came home one night with a Mr. Waters, an architect. Mr. Waters spread out some blueprints on the dining-room table, one roll for a red brick mansion in Newton, another for a red-shingled cottage in Sharon. The family stared at the plans in fascination. Construction, Mr. Waters said, could start whenever Sam wanted, since so many out-of-work carpenters and masons were available. The family could be settled in both houses by a year's time. Lenny and Shirley have recalled that they had never seen Sam happier. He would soon be the owner of *two* houses! And just twenty-three years before he was feeding the chickens in Beresdiv. Imagine! Jennie was somewhat less excited by this sudden bounty. It meant that she would have to move for the sixth time in five years. And besides she was thirty-three and pregnant again, the baby due at the beginning of 1932. At least there would be plenty of room for the new baby.

Contradictory feelings about the prospect of another child nibbled away at the fragile marriage. A couple of years earlier, Jennie had found herself pregnant, and, without telling her husband, she arranged for an abortion with a shady doctor in Dorchester. That impetuous decision, an act of panic, filled her with guilt and fear over what Sam, still quite Orthodox in his religious beliefs if Conservative in his temple membership, would do if he ever learned of it. He apparently never did, but the guilt and fear continued throughout her pregnancy in 1931. As far as Sam was concerned, he wanted another child, preferably a son, but he was experiencing grave doubts about his ability to govern a family. Lenny, in particular, showed signs of rebellion, with his consuming love of music (an alien and unproductive vocation if ever there was one) and no sign of interest in the beauty business. Shirley, only eight, was closer to her brother than to her father. They and their mother seemed to be another cabal against him and his principles, like the Resnicks. Perhaps a third child, another son, would be more like his father.

While Sam was generally ecstatic over the building of his two houses, he had, in effect, shot his wad on these enterprises, and worry about the fiscal future occasionally increased the tension in the Pleasanton Street house. One Tuesday morning, during Jennie's last month of pregnancy, they were all having breakfast in the kitchen. Tuesday was Bank Day at the Garrison School (in which students were taught the virtue of thrift by depositing some change in the classroom "bank"), and Shirley asked her mother for a quarter, as she had done just about every Tuesday of the school year. Jennie referred the request to Sam, who suddenly erupted in fury, shouting that all anybody ever wanted from him was money. He picked up a milk bottle and threatened to smash it. Jennie fled to the room destined to be the nursery and slammed the door. This further infuriated Sam, who tried to follow her, but Lenny spread-eagled himself against the door, defying his father and protecting his pregnant mother. Shirley screamed, burst into tears, and then ran to the "cold room." (Every Bernstein residence had a "cold room," an extra room that was never heated in the winter and was used as an occasional bedroom and place to hide.) At last, Sam, morosely embarrassed, calmed down and left for the office. But the effect of the Bank Day incident was traumatic, especially for Shirley, who felt that she was the cause of the whole ruckus. "It was the only time I remember him as physically violent," Shirley has said. "Usually, it was just deep silences and brooding."

Family Matters

The day I was born—in the early-morning hours of Sunday, January 31, 1932—Shirley and Lenny were left in the care of the maid, Agnes, as Sam rushed Jennie to the Evangeline Booth Hospital, in Boston. Agnes told Lenny that his parents had left for the hospital, and then offered to give Lenny explicit instructions in the original biological act that had brought about their abrupt departure. "Up to then, I had difficulty in finding out anything about sex, beyond street talk," Lenny has said. "It was never discussed in the house, naturally. We had no books on the subject. I was crazed with curiosity. I would look up 'childbirth' in 'The Jewish Encyclopedia,' the only encyclopedia we had at the time, but there wasn't much to learn from that." Agnes was another matter. However, Lenny was resolute —and terrified. Just as well, because soon after Agnes's offer Sam returned home from the hospital, awakened his children, and proudly told them that they had a baby brother. Lenny, who was in the middle of his first year at the Boston Latin School and had just that week been studying the poetic function of alliteration, suggested that the child be named Burton, since it went well, alliteratively speaking, with Bernstein. Sam and Jennie had already decided upon Bezalel as my Hebrew name. Burton seemed close enough to it, so Burton it was. For some reason, neither Lenny nor I was ever given a middle name.

The particular half-acre lot in Newton upon which Sam chose to build his dream house came into his possession because of his friendship with Ben Marcus, a fellow-member of the Mishkan Tefila congregation. Mr. Marcus had long since made his Roxbury-to-Newton move, and he convinced Sam that he should buy the lot next door. But the adjacent parcel of land was narrow, without room for a decent driveway. Don't worry, Mr. Marcus told Sam; we'll share my gravel driveway. It sounded equitable, but shortly after our great square mansion had been completed and we moved in, during 1933, the common driveway triggered a Bernstein-Marcus feud that lasted for eight years. The arguments over who should shovel snow from the driveway and who should replenish the gravel and who had let whose car block the right-of-way became so intense that Sam and Ben stopped speaking to each other. Although they attended the same weekly services at Mishkan Tefila, in Roxbury, they refused to ride in the same car to the temple. With deliberate timing (and much peering from behind curtains to see who had gone to his garage first to back his car out), they left separately for Roxbury, just minutes apart. Occasional shouting matches occurred when, by accident, they would confront each other in mid-driveway. After the 1938 hurricane, a major debate raged over a fallen tree. Their bitterness carried over into what was known as "*shul* politics"—the wrangling over petty matters in the administration of the temple and the selection of its officers. The feud was so bad in the late thirties that Sam forbade members of his family to have any contact whatever with the Marcuses. This edict was disagreeable for Lenny and me, especially. Lenny was entranced by Grace, the older Marcus daughter, who was a poet, a pianist, and an intellectual; I was in awe of Sumner, the Marcuses' only son, who constructed crystal sets and battery-operated intercoms. In both of our cases, Sam's stern prohibition was finally ignored. I discovered ways of sneaking into Sumner's basement workshop, and Lenny found places to meet Grace and discuss Oscar Wilde's poems.

The gravel driveway also happened to be the setting for my first clear memory. When I was about two years old, I was given a tiny tricycle for maneuvering about a grassy play area behind the garage. Once, when neither my mother nor the maid was looking, I decided to emulate my father and go for a spin on the road. I got as far as the slight, paved incline leading from the driveway to the street, and, losing control, tumbled onto Park Avenue just as a truck passed, missing me by inches. There followed in

75

rapid succession a howling of brakes, a white-faced truck driver, a screaming mother, a hysterical maid, alternating threats of punishment and embraces of comfort, and, finally, the scrubbing of my scrapes, cuts, and bruises with laundry soap and hydrogen peroxide. I can still smell that distinctly sharp combination of yellow soap and H_2O_2, and feel the stinging.

Newton in the thirties was a country suburb—especially the undeveloped section we lived in. Despite the happenstance of the truck passing just as I spilled onto Park Avenue, little traffic rumbled by. In my early years, much of that meagre traffic was horse-drawn—Hood Milk delivery drays, sidewalk snowplows pulled by steaming ponies, even private rigs. The area was, in the main, both genteel and Gentile. Broad meadows shaded by stands of first-growth beech and oak were not uncommon. Most of the houses along the gaslit streets were old, gracious, well-landscaped, and inhabited by moderately rich Protestants. A few Jewish families had settled there in the twenties, and, as more could afford the upward move from Roxbury, their number grew to a sizable minority of the population. Our house was neither old, gracious, nor well landscaped, but it was large—"an ark of a house," my mother called it, when faced with furnishing its ten sprawling rooms. Red brick on the outside and stucco-walled on the inside, it was constructed as sturdily as a bunker, and its bleak façade sometimes reminded visitors of one—more often, a W.P.A. post office. It contained servants' quarters, a spacious kitchen, a pantry, and a dining room, a library (Sam's retreat), several bedrooms (a master bedroom for Jennie and Sam) and bathrooms, a huge walk-in attic, and (the most fun for me) a maze of a cellar with a trunk room, a mysterious laundry room, and wondrous machinery, including a laundry chute big enough to hold a plummeting child. What the house lacked in charm it made up for in luxurious space— something exiles from ghettos valued above anything else.

Sam and Jennie

IN MY PARENTS' CIRCLE OF friends, there was a generally accepted hierarchy of economic station. The lowest man on this fiscal totem pole was the one of whom it could be said, "He doesn't have two nickels to rub together." That unfortunate was the worker most hurt by the Depression, barely surviving on handouts from relatives and odd jobs. Slightly better off was the man who "makes a living"—that is, gets by, feeds his family, and pays his bills when he can. Just above him was the "salary man," who held down a steady job. (A "government man," in this parlance, was a salary man with a more secure civil-service job, not dependent upon patronage.) Next was the fellow who was "in business for himself." He could actually be making less than the "salary man," but at least he was his own boss, a position commanding respect. When things went well for the person in that category, it was said that he "makes a *good* living" or is "comfortable." Then came the "professional man"—doctor, lawyer, teacher, clergyman (not an artist, however)—who fully deserved every penny he made, because he lived by his wits and talent. At the top end of the totem pole, in rising order, were the "a-dollar-means-nothing-to-him" man, the "he-has-money-to-burn" chap, the "well-to-do" fellow, and, at the very pinnacle (uttered with naked adoration), the "wealthy" gentleman. The word "rich" was never used. When you had truly made it in America, you were "wealthy."

During my childhood, I suppose we vacillated between "makes a *good* living/comfortable" and "well-to-do," although it was rarely said of Sam Bernstein that "a dollar means nothing to him." In the thirties, we had all the appearances of being well-to-do: the Newton house, the

Sharon house, a Packard sedan, a Plymouth Roadster with rumble seat, substantial furniture, a long succession of maids, and, for a short time, a West Indian butler-chauffeur-factotum named Zeno. But Sam never really let himself go monetarily. A man better suited to the world of business would have taken his profits and reinvested them; he would have risked capital, expanded, diversified. At the apex of Sam's success, he took only two modest fliers. He opened a branch office in Providence, Rhode Island, and closed it about six months later, when the manager and certain cash receipts disappeared. The harsh lesson he learned from that experience was, he said, to supervise everything personally and trust no employee completely— except, of course, the virtuous Abe Miller. On the other occasion, he hired a chemist to concoct various beauty-salon products, to be patented under the house label "Avol Laboratories." Only one product survived Avol's brief tenure—a white shampoo called "Fome," which was sold for many years in gallon jugs exclusively to hairdressers.

Sam had the wisdom to know that he was not a born businessman and that he had succeeded in commerce because of good luck and hard work, not because of his mercantile genius. As rewarding as the Frederics bonanza had been, it would not last forever, he reasoned. (He reasoned correctly. The cold-wave-permanent process came in around 1940 and replaced the cumbersome Frederics machines. Frederics machines still flourish in hair-styling shops in China, however.) Would whatever replaced Frederics or human-hair goods or the latest bob fad in the erratic beauty business be profitable? Probably not. Better to save for the rainy day, when reserves might be needed just to stay solvent. So the more money he had, the more he feared losing it—an attitude perhaps born in the Russian *shtetl*.

Once the euphoria of the new material possessions had waned, marital fights over money erupted again. In no way did Sam worship the golden calf—far from it, in fact; he took Biblical strictures against greed very seriously—but money itself emerged as a symbolic excuse for expressing his dissatisfactions with his marriage, his in-laws, his wife's friends, his children's alien way of life, his own dilemmas. It is no coincidence that in Lenny's short opera "Trouble in Tahiti" the husband and wife (named Sam and Dinah) bicker over money as a starting point for deeper quarrels. In the opening scene, Dinah sings, "Oh, by the way, my money's run low," and she and Sam are off on another hopeless domestic battle. And Dinah's suspicions about an affair her husband allegedly had with his secretary, Miss Brown, spring from a biographical incident. The malevolent wife of one of my father's employees once telephoned Jennie to hint that Sam was sleeping with a woman who worked in his office. It wasn't true—if the thought had ever crossed Sam's mind, it would have been obliterated by dread of a wrathful God and possible disclosure—but the mean tale reduced Jennie to sobbing and depression and renewed squabbling with Sam.

The money battles usually began with Jennie's requests for cash beyond her weekly stipend for household needs. Her timing for these requests was, at best, insensitive. She would ask him for an extra twenty dollars while, for example, driving him in the early morning to the station at Lake Street, from which a rackety orange trolley would hurtle him along, and finally under, Commonwealth Avenue to Boston. This tactic would spark a sullen, breast-beating dialogue, followed by an electric silence, which would sometimes last for days. If her approach was heavy-handed, her motive was selfless. The extra twenty dollars (or ten or five, or whatever she could scare up) were put in an envelope and sent directly to the Resnicks, most of whom had left Lawrence, where the mills and Pearl's real-estate business were hit hard by the Depression, and resettled in Dorchester. Their musty railroad flat, on Dorchester's Angell Street, housed Pearl, Samuel, Betty, Bertha, Dorothy (all three daughters unwed), and a scruffy dog, Prinny. (Joseph and Louis had their own families and were earning modest livelihoods in Lawrence by junk dealing and engraving, respectively.) Bertha and Dorothy continued to work in Sam's wig department, and Betty sold scarfs behind a counter at Stearns', in Boston.

The Resnick parents ran a tiny mom-and-pop candy store on Blue Hill Avenue, just around the corner from their apartment. The nickels and dimes the store gained for the family were scarcely enough to pay the rent, but for me the store was a child's fantasy come true. Crammed within the narrow cubbyhole were shelves, racks, and glass-fronted counters holding such items as newspapers (including Yiddish, Polish, and Russian journals), magazines (from *Photoplay* to *Superman*), cheap toys like sparklers and cap pistols, some canned goods and bread, and a seemingly limitless inventory of penny candy—crumbly halvah and stale, brittle spearmint leaves being my favorites. A sweating red-and-white ice chest emblazoned with the Coca-Cola legend contained every imaginable brand of soda pop (or "tonic," as we called it in Massachusetts), even birch beer and Moxie.

I was given the run of the store and allowed to claim any toy, comic book, or sugary edible within reason, for which my mother trebly reimbursed her father. My visits to the dream world on Blue Hill Avenue were also rewards for behaving bravely at Dr. Isadore Finkelstein's office nearby. Dr. Finkelstein was our all-around family physician—indeed, he had delivered me at the Evangeline Booth Hospital, and some years later, removed my tonsils while I lay chloroformed on our Newton breakfast table—and since I tended to catch colds easily I was taken every few weeks to "Dr. Finky" for inoculations called "cold shots." The cold shots did no good whatever (neither did my father's command to "button up your neck!"), but if I didn't cry when the hypodermic needle went into my arm my grandfather's candy store was mine to possess. I seldom cried. And it was in front of that wonderful store that, in the autumn of 1936, I saw Franklin Delano Roosevelt speed by in an open limousine, on his way to a campaign stop. There was opportunity for just a glimpse of that smiling, godlike figure in the center of an earsplitting motorcycle escort, but the exultant crowds along Blue Hill Avenue stayed in place still cheering and discussing the visitation for an hour after the President had passed. "That he would come to Blue Hill Avenue!" my grandfather said. "Isn't that something!"

Like the other working-class Jews in that throng, the Resnicks were among the oppressed of the Depression. My father, however, didn't quite see things that way. To him, the Resnicks were lazy, unimaginative, and wasteful of what they had. Wasn't it enough that he had married and was supporting in style their oldest daughter, employing two other daughters, and sending his in-laws checks in emergencies? (He didn't know about Jennie's weekly envelopes, or about our cast-off clothes and shoes that went to Louis's and Joe's families.) He was still irrationally blaming the Resnicks for all things dumb and ordinary, and for his marital difficulties.

The Resnicks' troubles grew steadily worse. One summer day in 1935, Jennie received a phone call at our Sharon house. After a long conversation, she walked into the kitchen and stood sobbing over the sink, her tears dripping freely into the drain. Alarmed, I asked her what was the matter, and she said that "Grandma Pearl had a shock"— her euphemism for a stroke. Since I had often been warned against sticking my fingers or odd implements into electric sockets, I assumed that my grandmother, who should have known better, was guilty of that dangerous error. (It was a long time before I would touch anything electrical.) Pearl's stroke had left her paralyzed on one side and unable to speak, which meant that she would have to be put in a nursing home, and Sam would have to foot the bill. He dourly obliged—there was no alternative, really, since everyone in the Resnick family worked and could not look after Pearl during the day—but his responsibility didn't last long. On August 25, 1935 (Lenny's seventeenth birthday), she died. It was a catastrophe for the Resnicks. Pearl had been the prime mover of the close-knit family, its source of spirit and survival. Her husband was irreparably wounded by her death. He continued to run the candy store, but without enthusiasm. His children cared well for the kindly, warm old man, and Jennie sent more envelopes than ever. But life without Pearl was not the same for him. Almost six years later to the day, he, too, died.

*I*T SEEMED THAT THE MORE success and security Sam acquired during the Depression, the more he was a casualty of his personal depression. All his old dilemmas were exaggerated, perhaps because he had more leisure time to stew about them. He suffered through the quandaries of his youth again, only now they were magnified by adulthood. What was his real role in life? Was he a businessman or a man of God? If he was truly a pillar of Boston commerce—like his idol and competitor, that magnificent Yankee Russell B. Tower—why couldn't he act and feel like one? Sam tried. Lord, how he tried! He joined the Pine Brook Country Club, in the belief that proper gentlemen of commerce (like Mr. Tower) should play golf, occasionally taking off a business-day afternoon for a round on the links. But, it turned out, Sam felt guilty about leaving the office early unless he was ill. Saturday was his Sabbath, which meant no golf, and somehow on Sunday he could rarely rouse himself for the drive to the club. Besides, he was inept at golf—at all active sports, for

that matter, except, perhaps, stick-hurling. His membership in Pine Brook lapsed after a year or so. He built a clay
tennis court on the Sharon property, but he was content
just to watch his children and their friends play, until
watching the mysterious game bored him silly. And even
before he moved to his swanker offices—in the Blake
Building, on Temple Place—in the early nineteen-thirties,
he unfailingly lunched at the Temple Place Thompson's
Spa, the preferred restaurant of Mr. Tower and dozens of
other distinguished Boston merchants, bankers, and lawyers. He lunched there on its bland, wholesome food for
twenty-five years; then, one cataclysmic afternoon, he discovered a burnt match in his rice pudding. He left Thompson's Spa never to return. Thereafter, he ate at Schrafft's,
a similarly "Yankee" restaurant near his office. (On special
occasions, such as important business lunches, he dined at
the Locke-Ober restaurant, a Boston culinary landmark,
but the rich food there upset his delicate stomach.) Try as
he might, he knew that he would never be a convincing
Yankee trader.

But, then, if Sam was not inherently a businessman, was
he truly a man of God? And, if so, what kind? With his new
status, he had deserted the Orthodox *shuls* and was immersed in the nigh-Protestant milieu of Conservative
Mishkan Tefila. However, something deep within Sam
made him uncomfortable there. An inner voice seemed to
warn him that Mishkan Tefila wasn't the real article, that
the pure faith of his fathers lay in traditional Orthodoxy.
Every so often, this inner voice badgered him into attending the ultra-Orthodox Crawford Street Synagogue, where
the women sat upstairs, and the men, almost invisible in
their prayer shawls, keened loudly, and not one syllable
was cut from the lengthy liturgical services. These visits
both purged him and, in the end, repelled him. True, he
felt closer to those traditionalists, but he could not bear the
airless, narrow world they represented—the world he had

fled in 1908. And Crawford Street was no place for him to take his family. A profoundly religious man, he felt at home in neither sect. The third possibility, Reform Judaism, with its hatless congregants, was absolutely out of the question.

Maybe Sam was more an intellectual Jew, a scholar rather than a devout participant. He never stopped studying the Talmud, and he sought the company of learned professors and rabbis. Yet what practical use could he make of their learning and their microscopic analyses of the Law? It was far too late for him to become a scholar-rabbi. The mystical call of the joyous Hasids, with their total commitment to their faith, was, well, more entertaining and uplifting than the dry hair-splitting of the scholars, but it was almost impossible to be a confirmed Hasid in twentieth-century Newton, Massachusetts, and also be the head of a modern American family. The swirling religious conflicts I observed in my father when I was a child were distilled for me then by his paradoxical rules for *kashruth*, the Jewish dietary laws. Food in our house had to be strictly kosher. Outside the house, we could eat anything we wanted—fried clams, broiled lobster, bacon and eggs, anything. It made no sense to me then; it makes no sense to me now.

When Sam's nagging quandaries simply became too much for him, he would sink into dark periods of melancholia. We could usually tell that these attacks of gloom and despair were coming on from the moment he walked in the door after a long day at the office. With hardly a word of salutation, he would remove his eyeglasses and his wristwatch, take the loose change from his pockets, deposit everything on the living-room mantelpiece, and pace back and forth on the Oriental rug until dinner was ready. Just before he sat down at the table, he would pour himself a shot glass of good Scotch, knocking it back in his customary Russian manner—neat and quick, with a small grunt.

Sam and Jennie

Dinner, aside from Lowell Thomas's newscast, was then conducted in almost total silence, the generally desired aim being to get the meal over with as soon as possible. Still brooding, Sam would return to the living room for more concentrated pacing, not even attempting to read his books or the newspapers, as he ordinarily did after dinner. At precisely ten o'clock, he would go for a twenty-minute walk. By ten-thirty, he would be in bed, without having said good night. "During his depressions, he felt so unloved, so isolated, so estranged from us all, it fed his melancholia," Shirley has said. "It made me frightened. I never knew whether he might whirl on us."

We were all frightened, and we all learned to stay clear of him during these bad spells, hoping they would pass in a couple of days, which they frequently did. On those occasions when they didn't, nobody was as frightened as Sam himself, who would then try his own remedies. One of his cures was to check himself into a sanatorium in Stoneham, Massachusetts, run by the Seventh-Day Adventists. (While there, he nimbly resisted their proselytizing and took comfort in their observance of Saturday as the Sabbath.) The massages, the steam baths, the scrupulous regimen, and the medical attention to him at Stoneham did him "a world of good," he used to say. He would arrive home in a slightly manic state, full of good humor and droll stories, ready to take on whatever life offered. So it was with his other panacea—a winter cruise to the Caribbean or Florida, on which he would sometimes take Lenny but never Jennie. The sea air also did him "a world of good," and so did the "getting away from it all"—meaning the corrosive contradictions of his life.

Jennie was of little help to him in sorting out and softening his dilemmas. Whenever she would try to talk things over with him, the discussion would end in snarls, slammed doors, and long silences. Increasingly, her concerns centered on her children (especially Lenny and his

music), movies (Anne Shirley was still one of her favorite
stars), thick romantic novels (such as "Anthony Adverse"),
and the companionship of her sisters and what my father
called her "*yachna* friends." (A *yachna* is a *yente* to the
tenth power, which is to say a virago of the coarsest type.)
Her best friend—and the one Sam disliked most—was Bessie Zarling, a widow who lived in a dreary Roxbury apartment and was crushed by her burdens. Since visits to
Bessie Zarling were often combined with visits to "Dr.
Finky" and the Resnick candy store, I witnessed several of
Jennie's sessions with her friend. Their meetings would
invariably begin with the once attractive woman opening
her apartment door just a crack, blinking her large, rheumy
eyes until tears welled, and then announcing with a pon-
derous sigh, "Oh, Jennie, I feel so blue." Bessie was a
kvetch, a chronic complainer. When it came to the question of who was feeling bluer, she consistently won out
over Jennie. Her beloved husband had died long before his
time; there were problems with her children; her income
was less than satisfactory; the plumbing was deficient; the
neighbors made too much noise; her gallbladder was acting
up; and so on and on. If my mother submitted an emotional complaint (I was supposed to be playing in another
room, but I overheard everything), Bessie lost no time in
relating a far more tragic story. With this curious protocol,
she provided a kind of safety valve for Jennie. No matter
how bad things might have been for Jennie at home, things
were always worse for Bessie Zarling.

*T*HE ASTOUNDING RISE OF
Adolf Hitler, the Nazis' persecution of the Jews, and the
inevitability of war in Europe intensified my father's spells

of depression. He read the news dispatches from Germany, and he listened to the grisly broadcasts of Hitler's speeches (and, from Detroit, Father Coughlin's radio exercises in anti-Semitism) with the sullen fascination of a condemned man. Sometimes Sam would want to discuss the grim events of the day with his family—or lecture on them, at Sunday-afternoon dinner—but as a rule particularly bad news would plunge him into another brooding silence. What we didn't fully understand was that an entirely new and frustrating conflict was erupting within him—one that was literally a matter of life and death: Should he take immediate steps to bring his close relatives still living in Russia to America and safety?

The potential danger to his brother, Shlomo, or Semyon, was not great. The brothers had attempted a fitful correspondence during the twenties and thirties, and Sam knew that Shlomo was as secure as any Communist functionary could be. In his few letters to Sam, Shlomo made it clear that he was living in adequate circumstances with his wife and young son, that he was enjoying the rewards of being a professional man in the workers' paradise, and that he would not trade his station in life for anything. (He also made it clear that it was not wise for Sam to write to him on stationery with the Samuel Bernstein Hair Company letterhead.) So Shlomo would not leave Russia, and neither would their sister Sura-Rivka. Sam learned that she was still living with her husband, Srulik Zvainboim, and their sons, in Mezhiritsh, which after the Soviet-German Nonaggression Pact of 1939 was annexed as a part of the Russian Ukraine. Although Sura-Rivka Zvainboim was considerably lower in the Soviet scheme of things than Shlomo, she was content to live out her life there. Of Sam's closest relatives, then, only his aged parents, Yudel and Dinah, still making do in Beresdiv, were left for him to fret about rescuing.

And fret he did. The essential element in his newest

dilemma was raw guilt. In spite of the Nonaggression Pact, Sam sensed that Yudel and Dinah would be prime victims of the Nazis; the pact would probably not hold up, and the Jews of the Ukraine would ultimately meet the same fate as the Jews of Germany and Poland. His parents' best chance for survival was to get on a neutral ship and sail to America as soon as possible. But would they be happy in America? They were old, and unchanged in their *shtetl* ways even after living under Communism for twenty-two years. Their presence would be a burden to him and a constant reminder of everything he had escaped from. But they were his mother and father, after all, and he possessed the power to give them life, just as they had given him life. He had the money and the influence to bring them to America; he knew from an exchange of letters that they would be willing to come. The only thing preventing their emigration was Sam's own selfishness, and that inescapable truth made him all the more guilty.

At last, a solution appeared. His sister Clara, who was divorced from her second husband and was operating a bridal shop in Brooklyn, offered to look after Yudel and Dinah if Sam would arrange for them to leave Russia. Clara would put them up in an apartment among their own in the Orthodox Brooklyn community of Williamsburg, far enough from Massachusetts so that Sam would see them infrequently. It was a workable arrangement. In the winter of 1940—while the British and the French were waiting uneasily for the Germans behind the Maginot Line, and the Russians were breaching Finland's Mannerheim Line —Sam contrived an escape for his parents. They would travel from Beresdiv to Moscow, and then take a train to Leningrad, where a ship, under neutral colors, would take them to New York. Once Sam had concluded these complex plans, it was as if a black storm cloud over his head had suddenly evaporated.

The immigration agency that handled this itinerary informed Shlomo that his parents would spend a short time in Moscow before sailing for America. The apostate son, who had rarely seen or communicated with his parents since he left home, agreed to put them up in his apartment. Their reunion in Moscow was tense but polite. It was the first time that Yudel and Dinah had ever been outside the Ukraine, and they were cowed by the great city and by the absence of Jewish tradition in Shlomo's household. Shlomo and his wife, Fanye, were uncompromising Communists, who had denied every remnant of their past. The old parents had lived long enough under the Soviet system to accept the situation, however grudgingly. The lack of mezuzahs on the apartment doorposts, the nonexistence of a single prayer book, and Shlomo's faulty Yiddish and Hebrew were loathsome to them, but vaguely understandable. One profanation was utterly unacceptable, though. Yudel suspected that Aleksandr, the five-year-old son of Fanye and Shlomo, was uncircumcised, which was the case with many sons of younger Russian-Jewish Communists. On the morning of his departure for Leningrad, Yudel could stand the suspense no longer. Alone with the boy in the apartment's kitchen, he managed to confirm his darkest suspicion. Without a second thought, he took a small carving knife and performed the circumcision rite then and there. When he and Dinah finally left for Leningrad, shrieks and curses followed them out the door. According to my father—who, with shaking voice, told me the story two decades later—they were lucky to get out of Moscow alive. The son and the father had disowned each other.

When the time came for Sam to greet his parents at the dock in New York—his first meeting with them in thirty-two years—he realized that he couldn't face the moment alone. Clara and some Brooklyn relatives would welcome them to Williamsburg, but Sam was the logical person to welcome them ashore after their voyage across the Atlantic that winter of 1940. Oddly, he did not ask Uncle Harry (Dinah's brother) or Abe Miller (Dinah's nephew) or Jennie or Lenny to accompany him on his emotional mission; instead he asked Shirley, then a senior at Newton High School, to go with him.

"Daddy invited me to go to New York with him, which was a very big deal for me then," Shirley said years later. "We went by boat, from Rowe's Wharf in Boston through the Cape Cod Canal and down to New York Harbor. It was very exciting—a great trip with my father. I had never been on a real ship before. The war in Europe was a faraway and unreal thing for me, and so was the idea of my Russian grandparents. Maybe that was the reason he chose me to go with him—I was somebody he wouldn't have to discuss the situation with too much. I don't know.

"Anyway, we stayed overnight in the Hotel New Yorker, which was pretty fancy in those days. It was a business-men's hotel, mainly, and Daddy used to stay there during his conventions and beauty shows in New York. I was really impressed. The next morning, we went down to a pier in Manhattan. I noticed that the closer we got to the pier, the whiter and more jumpy he became. He was terri-fied, actually, and I asked him what was the matter. He said that he hadn't seen them since he was sixteen, and he was frightened. Now, *that* was an impossible thing for me to grasp. I could barely conceive of Daddy's even having parents. The ship came in and tied up, and we stood near the gangplank. I think it was a Dutch ship. A lot of refugee types came down the gangplank, some of them rather ele-gant, all of them thrilled to be there. Daddy was searching every face like a man possessed. Suddenly, he spotted a little bent and bearded man with a high astrakhan hat on his head. It was a shock for Daddy. He remembered his father as a large figure, the way all children recall their parents after a long separation. But here was his father, bent over and shrunken. Beside him—and this was the big surprise—was a small, dainty, blue-eyed, alabaster-skinned woman wearing a babushka. She was so *little*. I could see that she had these enormous hands, which didn't seem to go with the rest of her. I was, of course, fascinated but not really involved. Daddy looked as if he were going to faint. Then there was this incredible scene: embraces, crying, a jumble of Yiddish. Since I didn't understand a word they were saying, I kind of tuned out and just stared. I must have been quite a sight to them. They probably didn't know what to make of their granddaughter, with her American clothes and her ignorance of their language. They were so tired and bewildered. It turned out they had eaten hardly anything on the ship, because the food wasn't kosher. They just ate some eggs and bread and drank tea—a lot of tea. They lived on tea.

"After they went through customs, we took them and their baggage by cab to Brooklyn, where Clara had fixed up an apartment for them. In the cab, Daddy tried to talk with them about the intervening years, but there was too much to say, and anyway they were too exhausted to say much. Dinah seemed so gentle and sweet. She just stared at me and smiled. She was not at all what I had imagined her to be. It's strange that I felt no great sense of family connection. They were from another planet, as far as I was concerned."

Sam settled his tired, tempest-tossed parents in their Williamsburg apartment, and, satisfied that they would be well cared for by Clara, the Brooklyn relatives, and the Orthodox community there, he lost little time in taking Shirley back to Boston. The emotional strain of the reunion was too much for him. He assumed that his parents would be happily transplanted to Williamsburg, where there was a synagogue on every block and Nazis were nowhere to be seen. He had done his filial duty. Before he and Shirley left, he saw to all their financial and bodily needs, including new, sturdy clothing for the winter.

One item of apparel—a heavy woollen overcoat with a linen lining—was immediately bought as an essential replacement for the old man's thin caftan, which he had worn from the moment he had left Beresdiv. However, Sam forgot about the Biblical stricture against the mixing of species—such as flax yarn and sheep fleece—and Yudel was gracious, or shocked, enough not to remind him of the abomination. Yudel put the offending garment away in a closet and refused to wear it, no matter how cold the weather. Since he also distrusted the plumbing fixtures in his apartment, he bathed in public baths operated by a local Orthodox center, as had been his custom in Beresdiv. On a particularly frigid day not long after his arrival in America, he returned home from the public baths with a hacking cough and a high fever. A doctor diagnosed his ailment as pneumonia, and suggested that he go to Beth Moses Hospital, nearby. Yudel adamantly refused; hospitals were as foreign to him as everything else in Moscow and New York City. For several months, he lay ill in a large bed, his shrinking body covered by a down-filled comforter. One of our young Brooklyn cousins, Blanche Brenner, was regularly brought to the apartment to visit him. "Long before they moved into Williamsburg, we heard so much talk about the great man and his wife coming to live in the neighborhood," she has recalled. "We were all told how learned and revered he was, a true man of God. We were so in awe of him that we tiptoed around the apartment, so he wouldn't be disturbed in his praying and studying. Even though he was small, he looked to me like a Biblical figure —like what I imagined God to be. Then he became sick, but, even wasting away in that big bed, he still looked like God."

Dinah—the "*mima*" (a variant of *mume*, or aunt), as she was generally called by her more distant relatives—was another story. As her husband's condition grew worse, the old woman who had seemed to Shirley so gentle and sweet turned into a harridan. She blamed America and its entire population for Yudel's plight—especially those Americans who were nearest and dearest. She and Yudel were the innocent victims of a grand conspiracy. No one was spared her denunciations, least of all her son Shmuel Yosef, who made several unexpected trips to Brooklyn to look after his parents. In her mind, both her sons were thankless creatures. And even Clara was unsympathetic, always insisting that Yudel go to a hospital. Finally, in the summer of 1940, Yudel lapsed into a coma and was rushed to Beth Moses Hospital, where he died within a few days. The guilt that Sam had exorcised by bringing his parents to America returned in triplicate as a consequence of their arrival. The steps he had taken to save their lives were covered with banana peels. His father was dead because of a cross-cultural misunderstanding, and his mother was inconsolable, praying fervently to return to Beresdiv. At last, there was nothing to do but bring Dinah home to his family.

It was an impossible situation from the first. We were still at our summer house in Sharon, where we stayed until Labor Day. When Sam alerted us by telephone to Dinah's imminent appearance, he also issued a rigorous set of instructions: meticulously clean the spare attic bedroom for her; double-check to make sure that there wasn't so much as a crumb of *tref* (forbidden impurity) anywhere in the house; warn Shirley and her girl friends not to wander about in their bathing suits (a display of bare female flesh was as bad as *tref*); provide special dishes; stock up on Swee-Touch-Nee Russian-style tea (which she drank in copious amounts); ban Lenny's piano playing on the Sabbath; and nail a mezuzah prominently to every single doorpost. (We had just one, on the sill of the front door.) The last commandment was the most difficult to fulfill. Mezuzahs weren't for sale at the Sharon hardware store. A special rush trip was made to a religious-articles shop in Boston in order to buy the necessary encased parchment scrolls, which were then nailed even to closet doorposts. Since the weather was oppressively hot and humid, Jennie bought some sleeveless light cotton dresses for her mother-in-law.

Dinah's arrival in Sharon took on the proportions of a state visit by Winston Churchill. My family—indeed, the whole Lake Avenue community—was scrubbed, sanctified, and purified when Sam drove up in his Oldsmobile, his mother next to him on the front seat. Of my first meeting with her, on that hot August day of my ninth year, I remember mainly a total inability to communicate anything at all. The dainty woman with an iron will gestured toward me to approach her. I obeyed, stiffly allowing her to kiss and hug me, and listened to her stream of questions in Yiddish, none of which I was able to answer. I was paralyzed. She called me "Bezalkele"—an affectionate diminutive of my Hebrew name, Bezalel—and thereafter the sound of that word on her lips sent me into a small panic. However alien she was to me, I am sure that I was positively extraterrestrial to her. I couldn't speak any of her languages, I ran around bareheaded, I never read a prayer book, I swam in the lake most of the day, and I flirted with cute Elaine Golden, who lived just down the street. Our sessions together—usually after dinner—would end with Dinah heaving sighs of disappointment at her worthless, heathen grandson. Soon, we learned to steer clear of each other.

The lack of connection between Dinah and me applied, in varying degrees, to her relationship with the rest of the family. I had never seen my father so consistently distraught. Lenny and Shirley also had trouble communicating with her; they tried, in desperation, sign language, Latin, French—anything. Only Jennie seemed to strike up a tenuous friendship with her, helping her bake challahs (braided loaves of egg bread) and allowing her to inspect every nook and cranny for traces of impurities. When

Dinah Bernstein, about 1950

Samuel and Pearl Resnick, early 1930's

Aunt Clara, Uncle Harry and Aunt Polly Levy, and Sam (seated), *about 1916*

Jennie, about 1917

Sam, about 1916

Sam and Jennie, engagement photograph, 1917

Annie and Abraham Miller, early 1930's

Jennie, Lenny, and Sam,
about 1922

Uncle Shlomo, with his wife, Fanye,
in Russia after the Second World War

Jennie and Sam, early 1930's

*Some of the Malamuds of Korets, in Russia before the
Second World War*

Aunt Clara, upon her graduation from nutrition school

Lenny and Shirley, 1933

Burtie and Shirley, 1932

Burtie and Mippy II, in Sharon, 1942

Burtie and Jennie, 1935

Sam, at an "affair," with klezmer, *late 1940's*

Sam and Lenny, about 1935

Lenny, in Wyoming, 1948

Lenny and Felicia, 1959

*Shirley, Lenny, and Burtie, at a
friend's house in Holland, 1950*

*Shirley and Lenny, in
Ireland, 1950*

Lenny, Felicia, Sam, Jennie, Shirley, Ellen, and Burtie, before Sam's
testimonial dinner at Boston's Sheraton Plaza Hotel, January 7, 1962

Sam and Jennie

Dinah eschewed her cool cotton dresses because they were sleeveless (and so permitted the bare flesh of her arms to be seen), Jennie cheerfully sewed in what I called "baseball players' sleeves." But it was clear that the uneasy arrangement could not last. The house was in disarray, and Dinah's reproachful sighs and harsh complaints were driving my father to search for new escape routes. Three disparate generations were under one roof, and the cultural collisions were horrendous.

An incident took place one night a few weeks after Dinah's arrival that just about put the cap on the situation. She had gone to sleep in her attic bedroom but awakened in the middle of the night, fearing that she had neglected to kiss the mezuzah before entering the room to retire. In the dark, she rose to correct her probably imagined oversight and fell down the attic stairs just outside the doorway, breaking her arm. The Sharon doctor was called, but Dinah resolutely refused to let him see her bare arm, despite her pain and my father's frenetic entreaties. As luck would have it, the doctor, George Hochman, was the son of our community's rabbi, Isaac Hochman. After much negotiation, a compromise was achieved: if Rabbi Hochman himself would appear and verify that the doctor was indeed his son and if the doctor could set her arm without observing her bareness any more than was necessary, Dinah would comply. The rabbi obliged, and his son put a splint on her arm. As far as Dinah was concerned, my father was to blame for the incident. That was the last straw. The next day, he arranged to have the *mima* move in with Abe Miller and his wife, Annie, who were living in Roxbury. When Dinah had left, Sam said, "I forgot how big this house is."

For Annie and Abe, life with their *mima* was, in Annie's typically direct words, "a Gehenna—a hell." Throughout the years of the Second World War, Dinah stayed with the

Millers, taking over their rooms and their lives. "Nobody could come to visit, because she had to have the living room all to herself," Annie has said. "By her, nothing was kosher—not even the chairs. She put newspapers all over my furniture to make them kosher. I was her slave: special big prunes she needed for her cooking, and I had to run out and buy them; pounds of butter and sugar for her cakes she wanted when they were rationed; her washing had to be done just so. Everybody was trying to poison her, she said. I showed her the food she was eating was the same I gave to my children, but, no, she was being poisoned. She had to make her own food to eat it. For this, Sam was paying me forty dollars a month expenses. No money was enough to take care of the *mima*. Finally, I got sick. The doctor said my pulse is fast, my blood pressure is high, I'm shaking all the time, so Sam puts her into the old people's home."

At the Hebrew Home for Aged, in Dorchester, Dinah continued to raise hell. Moris Citrin, the director of the home, was regularly on the telephone to Sam with an old or new complaint about Dinah's behavior: she had escaped by cab to the Millers' apartment in the middle of the night; she had accused another woman of poisoning her tea; she had washed a photograph of Yudel with soap and water, and when it streaked and faded she insisted that somebody had put a hex on her. At one point, she struck up a friendship with a distinguished old widower, a Mr. Levine, and there was some talk of a second marriage for both of them. Hopes ran high until Dinah concluded that she wouldn't be able to sit next to Yudel in Heaven if she remarried. Despite Mr. Citrin's frequent threats to evict her, she lived at the home—or occasionally at our house or the Millers' —until 1956, when she died, at the age of eighty-three. She was buried next to her husband in the Bernstein family plot at the Mishkan Tefila Cemetery, in West Roxbury, Massachusetts, six thousand five hundred miles from Beresdiv.

Sam and Jennie

*D*URING THE WAR, NEITHER Dinah nor anybody else in the family was able to learn the fate of those relatives still in Russia. From the news dispatches, however, one could hazard a grim guess. My father kept a map of Europe on a wall, with pins of different colors marking various armies' advances and retreats. In the summer of 1941, the black pins, representing the Nazis, were well into the Ukraine; the red pins, the Russians, were retreating east toward Moscow. I remember that one day my father told my mother that he had just heard on the radio about a fierce battle fought in Shepetovka, which was described by the newscaster as "an important railroad junction." She knew of no close relatives still there, but the news brought tears to her eyes. If Shepetovka fell, the *shtetls* nearby would be overrun easily. We were reasonably sure that Shlomo and his family would be safe in Moscow, but what about Sam's sister Sura-Rivka Zvainboim and her husband and sons, and the Malamuds of Korets? If the stories of summary executions of Polish and Russian Jews were true, they wouldn't stand a chance. As despised as Hitler was in 1941, nobody could bring himself to believe the stories were absolutely true. Such total evil was impossible—beyond human invention or perception.

Since there was no way of communicating with Sura-Rivka, the hideous thought was put aside. But as the war plodded onward it grew increasingly clear that she and the Korets relatives were casualties of the Holocaust. No one ever said so, exactly, but it was silently and resignedly understood. Sura-Rivka was just a cloudy memory to Sam —she was only an eight-year-old child when he left Russia —but at times he would talk about her lovingly. "She was so small, with blond braids and pretty blue eyes," he would say. "She didn't understand why I was leaving the house. I never really explained it to her."

At the end of the war, a letter arrived from Shlomo. He and his family were alive and well in Moscow. Sura-Rivka, as we feared, as we knew, had not been as fortunate. She, her husband, and three of her sons were murdered by the Germans about fifteen months after the Ukraine invasion. But—miracle of miracles—their oldest son, Mikhoel, had survived. Through later correspondence and from other sources, my father and I learned more about the miracle. Special S.S. units, the dreaded *Einsatzgruppen*—rather than the regular Wehrmacht—had been sent into the heavily Jewish areas of the Ukraine for a specific reason: so that there would not be the slightest hesitation about murdering every Jewish man, woman, and child encountered. No exceptions. The S.S. performed as had been expected. On the holiday of Succoth, five thousand Jews of Mezhiritsh—including Sura-Rivka, her husband, and their three younger sons—were herded into a brick factory outside the town and machine-gunned by the Nazis. However, Mikhoel had long since fled the area. At the time of the invasion, Mikhoel had just been graduated from the Mezhiritsh high school, and, defying his parents' wishes, he, with some friends, left home on foot for eastern Russia. In a recent letter, Mikhoel wrote me:

Father and mother tried to persuade me not to leave home: "If the time has come to perish, let us be together." But we younger people decided on a different path: "If the time has come to perish, let it be with a gun in our hands." At first, we made it on foot to the railroad station at Novograd-Volynsk, and from there we travelled by train to Kiev, and then from Kiev to the town of Aktiyubinsk, in northern Kazakhstan. There, I was mobilized with the Army reserves, and later entered the actual Red Army, participating later in the liberation from the Fascists of the Soviet homeland, Poland, and Czechoslovakia. I served as an artillery

soldier in an anti-tank brigade; for military sacrifices at the front
I was awarded the Order of Slava [Honor] and various medals.
. . . After the war, I was sent to Dnepropetrovsk for further duty.
In 1949, I was demobilized and started work at a chemical factory
as a vulcanizer. . . .

One could write a whole book about what took place during
the war. A full thirty-five years have passed since the ending of
that terrible war, yet I still remember the horrors of my war
years.

In 1947, Mikhoel married another Jewish survivor, Lena
Neishtat, of Dnepropetrovsk. A son—named Aleksandr,
like Shlomo's son—was born to them in 1948. My father
sent parcels of food and clothing to help them through the
postwar reconstruction years, and Mikhoel would answer
with letters of thanks written in Yiddish. Shlomo was loath
to write to Sam at all as American-Soviet relations wors-
ened.

One of Mikhoel's letters, dated November 8, 1948, re-
veals the simple gratefulness of a survivor. Translated, it
reads, in part:

DEAR UNCLE,

You can't imagine how much joy you give me when I receive
a letter from you. For aside from you and Uncle Shlomo, none
of my relatives have remained.

Dear Uncle! Write me frequent letters. Write me about your
children, about your wife, and about Grandmother.

In connection with the fact that our little boy turned 6 months
on 3.11.48, we photographed him and we're sending you his
picture.

I am very pleased to hear that your son is a famous conductor
and I imagine that you have a great deal of pleasure from
him.

I receive frequent letters from Uncle Shlomo in which he

sends you regards. And I send him your regards, too. Stay well
and give my regards to Grandmother, your wife, children, and
all relatives.

Hearty regards from my wife and son.

YOUR NEPHEW MIKHOEL

Again I want to thank you very much for the parcel. All the
clothes were very useful.

The deaths of Sura-Rivka, her family, and the last sem-
blances of *shtetl* culture were mourned by my family. But
no matter how many trenchant accounts of the Holocaust
I saw or heard through the years, the essential horror
somehow never really struck me in a personal sense. Perhaps it was because there were no actual funerals or grave-
stones or death certificates for the murdered; they had been
blithely, anonymously dispatched and then bulldozed
under or burned to ashes, to be forgotten. If an individual
Jew was not a breathing displaced person at the end of the
war, it simply meant that he had ceased to exist at some
point during the war. Seldom was a time or a place or a
circumstance of death noted for the record. Such, I assumed, was the case with our Malamud relatives of Korets.
Recently, however, while inquiring about Ukrainian *shtetl*
life at the YIVO Institute for Jewish Research, in New York
City, I came across a rare definitive accounting, a memorial called "The Korets Book." After the war, enough former citizens of Korets had discovered one another alive in
Israel to be able to set down, with hard knowledge, a final
tabulation of some of the deaths in their town. As I read
the pages, which were translated for me from the Yiddish
and the Hebrew, I noticed dozens of Bernsteins and Malamuds, but none of the given names were familiar. It wasn't
until I read an entry entitled "Family of Khedva and Ahuva
Malamud (Israel) and Abraham Malamud (America)" that
it all came home to me. The "Abraham Malamud (America)" was, of course, my cousin Abe Miller, the meek, just

Sam and Jennie

man who had toiled for my father ever since the Frankel &
Smith days. Under that heading was a long list:

Yisroel	Brother	Killed in Korets
Yudis	His wife	"
Tsile	Their daughter	"
Moyshe	Their son	"
Freydl	Sister	Killed in Mezhiritsh
Moyshe (the blacksmith)	Uncle of Altshteyn	Killed in Korets
Khasye	His wife	"
Shlomo	Their son	"
Reyzl	Their daughter-in-law	"
Mindl	Their granddaughter	"
Shmuel	Their grandson	"
Osher-Leyb	Their son	"
Mindl	Their daughter-in-law	"
Pesye	Their granddaughter	"
Menukhe	Their granddaughter	"
Kobke	Their son	"
Tove	Their daughter-in-law	"
Yosef	Their grandson	"
Nisn	Their grandson	"
Shayke	Their grandson	"
Khaye-Feyge	Their daughter	"
Froyim	Her husband	"
and their three children		
Zlate	Their daughter	"
Dvosil	Their daughter	"

After reading that death roster of people I never knew,
not only did I understand the Holocaust but I understood
—for the first time, really—what my family was.

The
Kids

*T*HE GENERATIONAL BREACH between my father and his parents had insidiously duplicated itself with Sam and his own children—"the kids," as we were collectively referred to by Jennie and Sam, no matter what our respective ages. It was another case of those proverbial chickens coming home to roost. The latest Bernstein parent-child breach began as a normal one, but it widened with alarming speed. By 1941, it was a small canyon, which caused Sam to feel all the more isolated from his family, the object of some sort of cabal. In his darkest, most depressed moments, he was given to saying, "I'm worth more dead to all of you."

The year 1941 was a critical period for Sam. Besides the guilt-producing burden of Dinah, there was the war, which also had an adverse effect on his business. Certain chemicals used in the manufacture of cosmetics were in short supply, and Sam feared that his business would be ruined. In 1927, he had received the New England franchise for the revolutionary Frederics Permanent Wave Machine, but the simpler cold-wave permanent, introduced around 1940, had just about finished off his once-lucrative Frederics franchise, and there was not the same exclusivity available for the several new cold-wave products. And he still wasn't able to acquire the prized Revlon line of beauty products. Lenny, having been graduated from Harvard, was in his second year at the Curtis Institute of Music, in Philadelphia. Shirley was in her first year at Mount Holyoke. What with business and tuition worries and little confidence in the future, Sam panicked. He put up for sale his dream castle—the Newton house—and enlarged and winterized the Sharon house. Education for his children was more important to him than any house.

When we moved to Sharon, in the summer of 1941, we moved for good. As we drove out of the driveway of the Newton house for the last time, I saw that my father was crying. I had never seen him cry before. He had probably lost his first-born son to the cryptic, foreign world of music; his daughter was thriving in the also alien, if essential, world of academe; his business—another child, so to speak —was faltering; and now his magnificent Newton house, the symbol of his success in America, was gone. Of his progeny, I alone was left around the house to comfort him in his middle age, and I was suddenly a resentful and withdrawn nine-year-old, furious that I had been snatched from my Newton home and friends.

In spite of his children's growing remoteness, Sam shouldn't have doubted our love. It was there, just as surely as his basic love for his own parents had been. But he doubted, and a nagging riddle possessed him: If I have given my kids every advantage, sacrificing for their education, why don't they "pull with me," why don't they see things my way, why don't I have *nachas* from them? It was that ancient Jewish principle of *nachas*—the inner gratification a parent feels from, say, a well-tutored older son's taking over the family business and settling down, or a bright daughter's marrying a nice boy, or a younger son's avidly following in the faith of his father—that spawned the riddle. The more one educated one's children, in order to have more *nachas* from them, the greater the gap that would ultimately deprive one of that *nachas*. It was a paradox peculiar to twentieth-century America, and there was no apparent solution.

The key figure in the generational split was Lenny—the first born, the scion who led the way for the others. From the beginning, he was special. Asthmatic, sensitive, intelligent, he left a deep impression on everyone, whether because of his chronic wheezing or because of his unmistakable precocity. Jennie knew that she had an unusual child. "When he was a sickly little boy and he'd turn blue from his asthma, Sam and I were scared to death," she has said. "Every time he had an attack, we thought he was going to die. I would be up all night with steam kettles and hot towels, helping him to breathe. If Lenny so much as sneezed, we would turn pale with worry. The first thing Sam did when he came home from the office, he'd say, 'How's Lenny?' But, sickly or not, Lenny was such a brilliant boy—always the leader of his gang, always the best in school."

And, she might have added, always the most inventive. For instance, when he was ten years old and the family was living on Schuyler Street, in Roxbury, he created an entire nation, with its own culture and language. Perhaps that in itself is not so remarkable, but how many such childhood creations have endured, even flourished, right up to the present day? Lenny and his best friend, Eddie Ryack, had been studying ancient history at the William Lloyd Garrison School, and, having been rather taken with the administration of the Roman republic, they decided to become consuls of a country called "Rybernia," an acronym of their last names. Of equal stature as the nation's leaders, they set up stringent rules for citizenship, mainly testing one's courage to undergo hazing techniques. The élite who passed muster and were admitted into this secret national society were Daniel Salamoff (a neighbor), Sid Ramin (another neighborhood boy, who is now the estimable composer-arranger), Harold Zarling (the son of Bessie Zarling, Jennie's weepy friend), and Shirley (a five-year-old mascot).

The culture and, especially, the language of Rybernia were rooted in prepubescent cruelty. Two children of a family in the neighborhood were nicknamed Sonny: the younger Sonny—called "Baby Sonny"—suffered from a speech defect and occasional fits of petit mal, during which he would become rigid for a few moments. With that distinctive heartlessness of youth, the Rybernians would stop Baby Sonny on the street and ask him his name, which came out of the poor child's defective mouth as "Babü Chonnü." If they questioned him long enough, he would go into a slight spasm and stand frozen and contorted. The giggling Rybernians would then imitate both his speech and posture, and thus a deformed, ridiculing patois was born, to go with the already established nation. Almost everything could be translated into some variation of Babü Chonnü talk; for example, the Rybernian named Salamoff became "Schlaudümopsch," and Shirley, the mascot, was "Mascodü." The Rybernian national anthem was sung, somewhat, to the words and music of "When the Moon Comes Over the Mountain," and it came out like this: "Ven da moonyagen come obyagen da montanü . . ." At the utterance of certain syllables, the anthem singers were compelled to freeze, like Babü Chonnü, into whatever positions they held at the moment.

The great era in the early development of Rybernian culture arrived a couple of years later with the family's move to more spacious quarters on Pleasanton Street, also in Roxbury. There, a large attic served as a clubhouse and "labjtobj" (laboratory) for the growing membership. Since Lenny's matriculation at the prestigious Boston Latin School, the national direction of Rybernia had veered toward modern science, and the labjtobj was used for such projects as distilling pure alcohol out of rubbing alcohol.

The Kids

"We set up some filched equipment, like a Bunsen burner and glass tubing, and proceeded to distill filched rubbing alcohol," Lenny has said. "When it came out pure alcohol —it never occurred to us to drink it—well, it was such a triumph, a miracle, that we were convinced a great scientific discovery had been achieved. We would then stand and sing the national anthem with reverence." (An earlier experiment was not quite as successful. Lenny and Shirley once wrapped two eggs in flannel cloth and placed them behind a hot radiator, in the belief that the eggs would hatch. When no immediate results were manifested, they forgot about the whole matter. A week or so later, a mysterious stench filled the house. Jennie solved the offensive puzzle, just when Sam threatened to move out, by discovering the wretched mess behind the radiator.) On Pleasanton Street, too, a new Rybernian song was created about the latest object of mockery—Agnes, the amorous maid. Its first line went something like this: "Agitated Aggü, the red-hot momyagen . . ."

The keen-eyed linguist will detect a certain foreign influence in the language, particuarly in the umlaut-"U" sound and the "agen" ending. Clearly, the accent of my father and many of his friends contributed to the development of Rybernian. In fact, anybody whose manner of speaking could be held up to ridicule—or, as Lenny sometimes put it, "anybody who talked funny"—was fair game for the language's evolution. Long after Roxbury, Eddie Ryack, and Baby Sonny were out of sight and mind, Rybernian continued to expand with added locutions inspired by people who talked funny. Uncle Harry Levy, in Hartford, for instance, always said, "I'll migh' " for "I might," and so "I'll migh' " became a standard expression. Annie Miller, the Polish-born wife of my father's cousin Abe, had a peculiar quality of speech that never failed to send the intolerant Bernstein kids into poorly stifled fits of laughter. In her plangent Polish tones, she might say, "I'm decoratink mitt new drepps, and I got to hank dem mitt rots and rinks and festooents." All streets were "straats" to Annie (Roxbury's Harold Street, near where the Millers lived, was therefore "Harralt Straat"), and, most deliciously of all, she referred to her husband, Abe, as "Ape." The word "ape," as proper or common or adjectival noun, became an important Rybernianism.

Another Polish influence was Alice, a later maid, who when asked the time would reply, for instance, "It smose snapas seven;" consequently, Rybernian Standard Time was always "smose snapas" something. A retarded boy in Sharon tended to mumble, against all physical laws, through his nose, and that anomaly opened a whole new speech pattern in Rybernian—the hangdog, embarrassed, barely decipherable declaration, usually of affection. Perhaps the strangest influence on the language evolved from Serge Koussevitzky, the conductor of the Boston Symphony Orchestra, who became not only Lenny's mentor but also his spiritual father. Koussevitzky was well known in musical circles for his charming butchery of English. An example that particularly amused his protégé "Lenyushka" was his use of a verb's past tense for the imperative; most memorably, he once shouted in despair at an erratic student conductor, "Took it a tempo *und* kept it!" So the misuse of the past tense took its place in our private lexicon. "How ya gonna did it?" is a common Rybernian question, often weighted with grave significance. Rybernian remains a living language. It is still developing, as any good living language should. While the changes and additions are no longer as cruel and derisive as they used to be, Lenny, Shirley, and I—the three of us well into our middle age—continue to call one another by our Rybernian names and to perform certain Rybernian rituals (when nobody is looking, usually).

I came on the Rybernian scene in the late nineteen-thirties, at a tender, impressionable age. I was then "Baudümü," and I still am. Lenny was "Laudü," but that monicker gradually changed to "Lennuhtt" (a late Annie Miller influence) Shirley, after her "Mascodü" stage, was called "Suyaumü," which through the years became "Hilee," for complex reasons. We three were—and, in a sense, still are —a closed society, with our own humor, culture, and language. Above all, our own humor. Others have tried— have even been encouraged—to break into this society, but, somehow, they have never quite made it. Of course, most people who have encountered our extremely restricted world have found the esoteric jokes and allusions boring (and with good reason), but some have made brave attempts to storm the walls of Fortress Rybernia. Lenny's wife, Felicia, came the closest, and his children and mine sometimes lapse into imitative Rybernian. But they never felt truly comfortable in that curious land. Jennie and Sam were privy to the language from its birth, and they occasionally sought to ingratiate themselves by using, with frightening inaccuracy, a word here and there. However, I suspect if they had picked up the spirit and text of the thing Rybernia would have immediately evaporated. The essential point of the private world of the kids was that it had to be a private world of the kids, sequestered from the parents. What we three had in fact achieved was the creation of an imaginary counter-family within the real family. Our Rybernian family had a father (Lenny), a mother (Shirley), and a child (me).

*I*T WAS PROBABLY JUST A COincidence, but a coincidence worth noting, that Lenny's invention of Rybernia and his love affair with music began in the same year. He had been attracted to the sounds of music before—the scratchy tunes emanating from Uncle

Harry's Victrola in Hartford, Hasidic ditties sung by Sam in his lighter moments or while showering, the quasi-operatic liturgical music of Sam's Conservative synagogue, Temple Mishkan Tefila—but not until he was ten years old, and living on Schuyler Street, was he overwhelmed by the idea of *playing* music. Aunt Clara, who had been living in Massachusetts for a while and had decided to return to New York, left her rickety upright piano with her brother Sam. (Clara, a natural, if untrained, musician, used her upright to pick out accompaniments for her vocal renditions of numbers like "Pagan Love Song.") From the moment the piano arrived in the Schuyler Street flat, Lenny was infatuated with it. The possibilities of sound it offered when he touched the keys obsessed him, and he drove the family to distraction by doggedly hammering out popular songs of the day and improvised tunes. In a reversal of the standard parent-child conflict over music, he had to beg for piano lessons, finally winning over his skeptical father.

The neighboring Karp family had two daughters, Frieda and Sarah, both of whom were piano teachers. Frieda Karp was selected to instruct Lenny in the rudiments of the instrument for a dollar a lesson. She visited the Bernstein apartment once a week and put her more than willing student through basic scales and such beginners' pieces as "The Mountain Belle" and "On to Victory." Lenny has said, "It was all well and good for a year or so. Frieda taught me to read music—I learned instantly—but before long there was a point when I was playing louder and faster than she was. I don't know if I was playing better, actually, but I knew that she couldn't teach me much anymore, since she was strictly for beginners. And so I sought an advanced teacher. On my own, I went to the New England Conservatory of Music—that's where you learn to be a good pianist, somebody had told me—and I was assigned to a Miss Susan Williams. She charged *three* dollars an hour, and all hell broke loose between Sam and me. He saw that things were getting serious, and he was not going to spend three dollars a lesson. So the fights began."

The real reason for the fights with his father was Lenny's scary dedication to his pianistic studies, not so much the expense of them. Money was Sam's instrument of control over his sometimes rebellious family; it provided a ready, if lame, excuse to deny whatever he didn't approve of. For Sam, the matter was clear-cut: his son would be suitably educated and then join him in his business one day. The one possible exception to this plan would be if Lenny had a religious calling; then Sam could boast of another scholar-rabbi, in the long Bernstein tradition. Under no circumstances, however, would Lenny be a musician. A musician to Sam was a *klezmer*. The *klezmer* was an impoverished musician, usually a fiddler, who wandered from *shtetl* to *shtetl*, playing at weddings or bar mitzvahs for a few kopecks, some free food and wine, and a night's lodging. In Sam's eyes, he was a disreputable character of the Old World, a rootless profligate who would die young of starvation or the worst diseases. The American version of such a person wasted his life away playing in cocktail lounges or with dance bands. Where would the *nachas* be in that? Great pianists were famous Europeans who came to America and performed with orchestras conducted by other famous Europeans. American Jewish boys had no chance in the field of serious music.

Jennie, though, was on her son's side when it came to the question of music, and that caused further marital resentments. Sam's nightly bellowing of "Stop that damn piano!" was balanced by Jennie's quiet encouragement. She, who as a child had followed strolling *klezmers* to the far reaches of Shepetovka, loved music, and she loved the idea that her son was capable of making pleasing sounds on a piano in her very house. (When she thought that nobody was listening, she would steal to the piano herself and play the one simple piece she had learned by heart—

"Dolly's Waltz," it was called.) It didn't occur to her that music would most likely be an unrewarding profession for her son. But Sam was the master of the house, and he decreed that he would pay for no more lessons at the New England Conservatory.

Lenny, it turned out, was just as stubborn as his father. His passion for music was so intense that he could not be dissuaded. To finance his lessons, he contrived to find occasional jobs in pickup dance bands and to give elementary piano lessons to children not much younger than he was. Before long, a saxophonist, a drummer, and Lenny had formed their own group and were performing at weddings and bar mitzvahs for a few dollars each. Sam's dreaded *klezmer* nightmare seemed to be coming true in spite of everything. For two years, Lenny paid for his own lessons with Miss Williams, and her torturous method of instruction—keeping the fingers bent over the keys, but with no third knuckles showing—almost convinced Lenny that perhaps the beauty business was better, after all. Meanwhile, Sam, although impressed by Lenny's initiative, was almost convinced that once his son got this piano playing out of his system he would turn to more promising interests, like the family business. A truce was declared, and Sam even contributed some money toward the lessons.

Strangely, it was Sam who took Lenny to his first concert ever—a Boston "Pops" benefit for Temple Mishkan Tefila, when Lenny was fourteen. It was also the first real concert Sam had ever attended, and the "Pops" performance of Ravel's "Boléro" had a devastating effect on both of them. While Lenny's musical tastes soon transcended the "Boléro," Sam continued for many years to read all sorts of programmatic and philosophical messages into the work. He would even attempt to intone it from time to time. It was undoubtedly his favorite piece of music. Not long after the "Pops" concert, a business friend gave Sam two tickets to a piano recital by Rachmaninoff himself, in Boston's stately Symphony Hall. Again, he asked Lenny to go with him. "It was a very severe program, with an abstruse late Beethoven sonata," Lenny has recalled. "Sam didn't understand it at all, but he suffered through it. I was thrilled to pieces." It is hard to believe nowadays that Lenny first attended a formal concert at the ripe age of fourteen—an age by which Mozart had already performed in several concerts throughout Europe. "I was not a prodigy, by any means," Lenny has said. "I didn't really know about such things as concerts. It was so provincial of me. I lived in the city of Boston, for God's sake!"

When Lenny had just about taken his fill of Miss Williams and her paralyzing method, he was persuaded by a musical friend that he should have a first-class piano teacher—perhaps the renowned Heinrich Gebhard, the finest in Boston. Lenny felt that he wasn't yet ready for that giant step, but he saw no harm in auditioning for Gebhard, although he would have to scare up twenty-five dollars for the audition fee. (Gebhard's lessons were priced at an astronomical fifteen dollars apiece.) The distinguished German concert pianist, who had a boxer's cauliflower ear, listened politely to Lenny's stiff, no-third-knuckles-showing rendition of his modest piano repertoire. Then he said that while the musicality was there, the technique and preparation weren't. Gebhard suggested that Lenny should be instructed by the best of his assistants, Miss Helen Coates, a prim lady from Rockford, Illinois, who had once studied with Gebhard herself and who charged only six dollars a lesson. Every so often, Lenny was told, he would have a special session with the master, who would appraise his progress. "When Sam heard about this new arrangement, he screamed bloody murder," Lenny has said. "There would come these terrible diatribes about the *klezmer* again, that the *klezmer* was no better than a beggar, that I would end up playing in a trio in the palm court of some hotel lobby. Education, by all means—but *practical* education." As a result of Sam's renewed opposition, Lenny had to play in more dance bands than ever to pay for the expensive lessons with Helen Coates.

Lenny's new piano teacher immediately recognized the musical gifts of her young student, and his musical intelligence as well. She put him through a stern regimen of scales and études, but she also encouraged his natural bent for music in general, including his own highly derivative compositions. She was so taken with Lenny that she allowed the one-hour lessons to spill over into two hours, the extra free hour sometimes spent wading through piano scores of operas—a fresh infatuation for Lenny, which Shirley happily shared by shrieking various roles with him at home. Finally, when Lenny was eighteen and at Harvard, he was deemed ready for Gebhard. Sam was somewhat more forthcoming with financial help, but Lenny could now make a decent income by giving piano lessons to his fellow-students. Gebhard soon fashioned him into a professional musician. As for Helen Coates, her interest in Lenny never flagged. Since 1944, she has been his loyal, efficient administrative assistant, and she probably knows more about Lenny than he knows himself.

As Lenny's talents bloomed, so did Jennie's fascination with those talents. Teen-aged Lenny gave her life new meaning, just as infant Lenny had. His music took her mind off her unhappy marriage. She would go with her son to Boston Symphony concerts, waiting in line for rush tickets and then climbing to the highest reaches of Symphony Hall. She basked in music, even if she didn't understand much of it—especially "those moderns," as she called them. Some of her enthusiasm rubbed off a little on Sam. The fights with Lenny over music continued, but Sam made it clear that he objected to music as a vocation only. Lenny has recalled that Sam would say to him, "You know, you can play the piano all you want. It's a wonderful thing to come home at night and relax at the piano after a hard day. But if you're going to be a *mensch* and support a family, you can't be a *klezmer.*" Sam hardly admitted it, but he was deriving a certain measure of *nachas* from his son's musical gifts. He evinced some pride at a student recital in Gebhard's studio as Lenny received the warmest applause. And when Lenny was asked to perform for the Mishkan Tefila Brotherhood dinners the father of the talented young pianist did not reject the congratulations of his *shul* brothers. On one of Sam's cruises to the Caribbean and on a later cruise to Florida, he took Lenny along. Since a piano was standard equipment on cruise ships, Lenny obliged the passengers with pop tunes, musical pranks (his favorite was playing a popular melody as, say, Bach or Beethoven or Rachmaninoff would have written it), and light classics. The most requested light classic was something generally, and inaccurately, called "The Hungarian"—actually a piano version of the Rumanian composer Grigoras Dinicu's "Hora Staccato." The cry of "Play 'The Hungarian'!" from our parents' friends would haunt Lenny for years. When he was a more accomplished pianist, he'd give them the real thing, like a Liszt "Hungarian Rhapsody."

Increasingly for Sam, there was satisfaction in being the lucky father of such a versatile, entertaining son. And at one point in the late nineteen-thirties Sam even found a way to mix business with Lenny's music. He sponsored a weekly fifteen-minute radio program called "Avol Presents . . ." on a Boston station, to promote the short-lived Avol Laboratories beauty products, which Sam had hired a chemist to concoct. The artist that Avol invariably presented was Leonard Bernstein at the pianoforte, running through light classics like "Malagueña" and, of course, various "Hungarian"'s. Still, playing the piano was no life's work for any son of Samuel J. Bernstein.

*D*URING LENNY'S DIFFICULT
teens, his most carefree times were the summers spent in
Sharon. *Sharon.* For me, the name evokes a maelstrom of
sensations:

The smell of Sea Breeze, a camphoric liquid that my
father sold wholesale to hairdressers and believed in as an
almost magical panacea, for ailments ranging from the
common cold to a sprained ankle. Pale-green bottles of Sea
Breeze were in each bathroom and bedroom and on each
porch of the Sharon house, for liberal use as mouthwash,
gargle, hair tonic, astringent, antiseptic, disinfectant, lini-
ment—anything. "It kills the germs," Sam would proclaim,
pushing the omnipresent bottle toward some complaining
family member or guest. What it was certainly best for—
and the reason I associate the smell with Sharon summers
—was healing the angry welts left by the notorious Sharon
mosquitoes, which attacked at dusk with a ferocity I have
never experienced elsewhere. The camphor in Sea Breeze
also fended off the less vicious of the breed. (Sam's early
faith in Sea Breeze proved to be well founded. I notice that
the product is currently for sale in drugstores and is adver-
tised on television.)

The sound of motorboats—especially mine—buzzing
about the lake like crazed water bugs, and the accompanying shouts of irate fishermen in anchored skiffs and sailors
in rocking sloops. And, punctuating all that racket, my
mother's daylong command to me: "Come out of the
water, your lips are blue!" And the cries of other mothers
warning their young about bloodsuckers, approaching
thunderstorms, and too many Milky Ways before supper.

The incredible sights and sounds of my father and his
friends arguing over *shul* politics or playing boisterous pi-

nochle on some screened-in porch, their rages and amenities couched in the comic locutions of middle-class Jews straddling the Old World and the New.

The tastes of the post-*shul* Saturday morning *kiddush*, a feast celebrating the Sabbath, prepared with loving care every week by a different resident of our Sharon summer colony, informally known as "the Grove." Chopped liver, presented in a dozen ingenious ways; herring—creamed, *schmalz*, and pickled; *taiglach*, sweet and gooey lumps of dough; *knishes* of all shapes and sizes; tiny matzah balls, impaled on colored toothpicks, with red and white horseradish; gefilte fish, the Grove's staple; pickled tongue, corned beef, chicken, turkey—all neatly sliced and laid out on salvers; fresh vegetables, with or without sour cream; pickles, sweet and sour and garlicky; hillocks of cole slaw and potato salad; gallons of a red wine that tasted like Karo Syrup; siphon bottles of Seltzer, and colorful quarts of orange, lime, cream, grape, and root-beer sodas; apple strudel. All this set on white tablecloths covering wide boards supported by wooden horses, in somebody's sunny back yard.

The fearsome touch of my grandmother Dinah when she came to Sharon for her short, disrupting visit. The rough but pleasant feel of a freshly laundered cotton sweatshirt on my freshly showered sunburned back.

My father had chosen the small lakeshore town, about twenty miles south of Boston, for our summer home (and for three years our year-round home) as a result of a July rental there in 1931. Not many country towns within feasible commuting distance of Boston were open to Jews in those days, either for vacations or for permanent addresses. The Sharon natives, mostly "swamp Yankees" who then were in difficult economic straits, sold their scrubby, unproductive land to the strange city people—land abutting Massapoag Lake, a flooded iron-ore mine that had supplied metal for Civil War cannon. Besides the availability of acreage on Lake Avenue, Sam was instantly entranced by the clear, piny Sharon air, the frigid, sprawling lake, and the companionship of people just like him—immigrant Jews who had made it in America. The Grove was, in effect, a middle-class American *shtetl*.

Each Sharon neighbor had a tale to tell not unlike my father's. They had come from Russia, Poland, Hungary, or, in a few instances, Germany, and they had sweated as laboring apprentices until they arrived in leather goods, furniture, ladies' ready-to-wear, groceries, fur, insurance, and, in one whispered-about case, bookmaking. According to their own hierarchy of economic station, they were, in the main, "well-to-do." A couple of the younger men were still in the "makes-a-*good*-living/comfortable" category, but they were scampering up to the next rank; a couple of the older men, whose grocery stores had expanded into supermarket chains, were actually "wealthy," and they were regarded with appropriate awe. Almost all of them lived most of the year in Brookline or Newton; a few still held on to their houses in the better parts of Roxbury. They were a tightly knit, neighborly, backbiting, feuding, forgiving, gracious, vulgar, devout, banal, parochial, charitable, fearful, stalwart community—or, as the old saying goes, just like other people, only more so.

The residents of the Grove so affected me with their mishmash of qualities and foibles that they served as the basis for some characters in my first short stories, compiled in a book called "The Grove." When the first story appeared in print, I received a letter from a woman who was a niece of one of the community's more eccentric individuals—Morris Finn, a beefy, scowling, blustery veteran of the Spanish-American War, whose usual attire was bathing trunks not quite long enough to cover his underpants, scruffy sneakers, and an undersized undershirt. His niece, a New Yorker, had been a perennial summer guest at the Finns' Sharon cottage. She wrote me that her uncle, "the

most unsophisticated and crudest of mortals," who cared
mainly about his asthmatic Boston Terrier, Teddy, and
fishing, "could make the best blueberry muffins and fry the
best fish you have ever eaten," and her letter continued,
"He'd go fishing very early, come home, clean the fish, fry
them, bake the muffins, and then invite me to breakfast. I
can't remember anything tasting as delicious. In the years
which have followed his death, I haven't thought too much
about him, but when I do, surprisingly enough, it isn't of
his boorishness or ill manners, but of his generosity with
those breakfasts. And I'm glad of that. Somewhere beneath
that long underwear, there was a heart. There must have
been! And wasn't he a dead ringer for Wallace Beery?"

I doubt if any summer visitor to the Grove ever forgot
the place and its people. Every guest—whether child or
adult, male or female, Jew or Gentile—was obliged to attend at least one weekend service at the Congregation
Adath Sharon, the quasi-Conservative synagogue founded
in 1930 by the two dozen or so original families in the
colony. Until 1942, when a new *shul* was constructed, on
Harding Street, the congregation met in the small cottage
of Rabbi Isaac Hochman. What stranger could fail to be
captivated by the chaos of those services? The droning in-
comprehensibility of Rabbi Hochman's Hebrew litanies,
mumbled through a scraggly salt-and-pepper beard. The
ancient rabbi's interminable sermons in Yiddish, beginning
with his curious salutation to the officers and membership
("Praziden . . . Vize . . . Treja . . . Secreta . . . Membekes
. . .") and ending, it seemed, in midsentence, shocking
the dozing congregation to embarrassed attention. And
those officers—slick, handsome Benjamin Sacks, the un-
conquerable president and undisputed leader of the Grove;
portly Samuel Pearlman and stone-deaf I. M. Kaplan, vice-
presidents; moody, erudite Samuel J. Bernstein, treasurer
—all with their own concepts of how a proper service
should be conducted, sometimes quibbling over protocol

during a particular ceremony, and succumbing to the heat and tension by resigning on the spot or refusing to speak to opponents until peace was negotiated. Unforgettable, too, were the spontaneous, prayerful assemblies whenever one of the Grove's sons went off to war, or the equally spontaneous and prayerful celebrations when a major victory was announced or a son came home.

Of all the guests who paraded through our Sharon house, Aunt Clara was by far the most memorable, my grandmother's abortive visit notwithstanding. My father and his sister had not been close since their days in Beresdiv. There must have been some chemical antipathy between them; even Sam's help in bringing Clara to America and in establishing her Brooklyn bridal shop didn't improve their relationship. She was always "crazy Clara" to him. After a marriage soon ended by her husband's death in the influenza epidemic of 1918, she married a brutish poultry-man named Goldman, with whom she lived in misery on his Massachusetts farm. She was so tormented by Goldman that she suffered a nervous breakdown and was committed to a state mental hospital. Sam visited her there as often as he could summon the courage. The visits ended badly—Clara screaming about the food and living conditions, nurses taking her away in a straitjacket, Sam retreating in despair. His epithet "crazy Clara" took on a whole new meaning for us: for a while, we actually believed there was insanity in the family. Her physical health collapsed, too. She became diabetic, almost blind, and consumptive. A doctor told her that she had just six months to live.

At last, Clara was discharged from the mental hospital and was granted a divorce from Goldman. Sam viewed with dismay both of those actions; as far as he was concerned, she was still crazy, and she was also a divorcée, a fallen woman. And she was the source of that damn upright piano, which had caused such turmoil in his house. But he grossly underestimated his sister. After her release

from the hospital and Goldman, she returned to Brooklyn
and discovered vegetarianism, enrolled in a special dietetic
school, and emerged as a bona-fide vegetarian nutritionist,
with all her physical and mental ills miraculously cured.
Clara reopened her bridal shop and remarried, happily.
She had saved her own life, but in her brother's eyes she
was still "crazy Clara."

To the rest of us, she was, I suppose, also "crazy," but
only in the figurative sense—unconventional and perhaps
a bit tetched. Her yearly visits to Sharon were tumultuous,
hilarious occasions for us and the entire community. Without receiving a formal invitation, exactly, she would send
word that she was arriving on a specific train at Providence,
Rhode Island, and we were expected to meet her there. My
mother (never my father) would drive to Providence at the
appointed time, and there she'd be, her homely, thick-
featured face beaming as she struggled with assorted rope-
tied bundles and cartons—her "heckle-peckle," as she
called them—which she insisted on carrying to the car all
by herself, as proof of her reborn vigor. Indeed, she was as
strong as an ox, a vital testimonial to vegetarianism.

Once she had unpacked her heckle-peckle, we knew that
the Sharon house would be turned inside out for the duration of her stay—usually a week, my father's absolute
limit. The bundles and cartons contained, first and foremost, an enormous electric juicer, and then all the edibles
that went into the juicer: organically grown citrus fruits,
beets, lettuce, celery, leeks, tomatoes, and various exotic
legumes that nobody had ever heard of. She would order
"everybody out from the kitchen" and begin to prepare the
evening meal; to wit, soybean patties designed to look like
hamburgers, wheat-germ hash, a bitter, almost drinkable
vegetable purée from the juicer, and raw mint for dessert.
Examining my skinny frame, she would declare that she
must "push citrus" on me to ward off colds and "flush the
kidneys." Shirley and Lenny needed "vitamin concentrates

and natural sugars" for their adolescent complaints, and Sam and Jennie should "take roughage for the stomach." I'm sure she was right, and it was all great fun—for the first two days, at any rate. Then we kids would discover each other sneaking off to Harry Horton's nearby variety store for some of his exquisitely greasy hot dogs, stale Hostess cupcakes, super-sour pickles, frozen Milky Ways, and Orange Crush sodas. Sam survived by eating large, meaty lunches at Thompson's Spa in Boston. At the end of her week's stay, Clara graciously permitted us to go out for a real dinner at a restaurant in Foxboro, where the nearest movie theatre was. From the quarts of citrus she pushed on me—pulverized, with the rinds and pulp, by that incredible juicer into the consistency of pea soup—I developed a loathing for fruit that lasted for years. And I still caught too many colds.

Clara, like many inspired health enthusiasts, tried to proselytize everybody she met. She found a lot of candidates in the Grove, not only for her vegetarian regimen but for her exercises. She would enlist squads of overweight women and men to follow her example in "bending and stretching," down by the beach or off in our apple orchard. A few became dedicated converts. She encouraged one and all to accompany her on "dew walks," taken at dawn in the fields and pinewoods. Her dew walks were for communing with nature and for practicing what she called "inner breathing." Her dawn awakenings of my family and the whole community gave my father new cause for fury, but he had to admit that it was quite something to see a long line of bleary-eyed neighbors imitating Clara as she danced and pranced through the dewy fields and woods, breathing inwardly and often singing outwardly. Sam, however, put his foot firmly down when Clara organized an all-female nude sunbathing group on our open solarium, above the sleeping porch. I was sorry about that, because it provided some fascinating moments for me and my young friends.

The Kids

Lenny felt a special affection for Aunt Clara, and she for him. He was "my dear nephy," as she always referred to him, and "a regular music genius." Clara worshipped music in any form, which further alienated her from her brother Sam, and she pushed music as a career on Lenny as much as she pushed citrus on me. Of course, pushing music made her seem all the crazier to Sam. "I've long had a theory that Aunt Clara was potentially a great Wagnerian soprano," Lenny has said. "That voice of hers could shatter glass. I'll never forget her singing 'Pagan Love Song' and 'Eli, Eli,' while I accompanied her on the piano. What musicality she had! Imagine what she could have been with a little training and encouragement! I think of her now with much emotion, even though we laughed at her then, and I'll forever be grateful to her. She loved me so much, and I loved her. I could never understand why Sam hated her. I guess he was constantly embarrassed by her." After her third husband died, Clara left Brooklyn and her bridal shop for Florida, where she died almost two years to the day after Sam's death. (She was born two years after him.) Perhaps her sweetest vindication in life was the signal success in the music world of her "dear nephy."

Aunt Clara was not the only Sharon guest who embarrassed Sam. During his Harvard years, Lenny would bring several college friends—budding poets, writers, musicians—home to Sharon for weekends by the lake. They were all "crazy artist nuts" to Sam, who sulked about the house until they departed. Their presence strengthened his conviction that the world of art was no place for Lenny. Perhaps no friend of Lenny made a wilder bohemian impression than Adolph Green. Lenny had once worked as a music counsellor at Camp Onota, in western Massachusetts, where he mounted a production of the Gilbert and Sullivan operetta "The Pirates of Penzance." A swarthy, prognathous lad from the Bronx, Adolph Green had been invited to the camp to play the role of the Pirate King, and

125

Lenny and Adolph became instant friends, each of them entranced by each other's sense of humor and knowledge of music. Green's musicality was, and is, extraordinary because he never received formal musical training. He is capable of performing—a cappella and with every orchestral instrument outrageously imitated—just about any symphonic work, classical or modern, down to its last cymbal crash. At Camp Onota, he passed Lenny's rigorous testing on obscure-themes identification, and an enduring friendship and collaboration was born. (The collaboration, with the addition of Betty Comden, later produced the Broadway shows "On the Town" and "Wonderful Town.") When Lenny invited Green to Sharon, they would sit around the house for hours, quizzing each other on, say, Beethoven scherzi and inventing brilliant musical parodies while Sam stewed and paced. "Who is that nut?" he'd say to the equally bemused Jennie. "I want him out of my house!" Years later, both Sam and Jennie grew to have sincere affection for Adolph Green (and other unconventional friends of Lenny's), but Sam, unlike Jennie, never really came to understand Green's special quality and talent— just as he never really understood his own son's or Clara's or, for that matter, any artist's.

The reason Lenny was able to mount an operatic production on slim pickings at Camp Onota was that he had a lot of practice in Sharon. At the start of one of his early summers there, when he was fourteen, Lenny conceived a presentation of Bizet's "Carmen" employing the available local talent pool, such as it was. However, Lenny's conception—coauthored with a Boston Latin School classmate named Dana Schnittkind—was a domestic version, with the boys playing girls' roles, and vice versa. Apart from that, the Carmen-Don José-Escamillo plot line stayed pretty much the same. "In our innocence," Lenny has said, "it just seemed terribly funny that Dana Schnittkind, who already had a dark, heavy beard, should play Micaëla, that tender, loving creature, and that I, out of sheer ego, should play Carmen, and that my girlfriend at the moment, Beatrice Gordon, should play Don José. As I recall, Rose Schwartz played the bullfighter, Escamillo. Since most of the people we could find for the chorus were girls, we had what turned out to be an all-male chorus sung by females, costumed as little old men wearing yarmulkes. We borrowed evening gowns from Mrs. Finn, and the wigs were supplied by none other than the Samuel Bernstein Hair Company. I played the piano, except when I was on stage as Carmen; then Ruth Potash played. The score was very simplified, with lots of cuts, and our version of the libretto was full of private jokes and allusions to Sharon. Because we cut and changed the story, the audience had to be filled in on what was going on, so Dana Schnittkind and I wrote a prologue, which was recited by Shirley, who was just nine years old and had some teeth missing in front. Poor little Shirley. She had to open the show cold, a terrible burden for a kid—for anybody. But she did it very well—memorized her lines and came out and spoke the prologue."

On the evening of the single performance (twenty-five cents admission), the entire Grove population appeared at Singer's Inn, Sharon's lakeshore resort hotel, whose dining room had been transformed into a stage, with bedsheets serving as curtains and drops. Singer's Inn itself became a part of the libretto, as did a renovated toreador who sang, "Herring I can eat with appetite/Ten bulls a time I can fight." The audience was treated to the spectacle of Shirley, in a new party dress, quaking and gamely lisping her prologue; Lenny, in black wig and mantilla, alternately playing the piano and singing Carmen; Dana Schnittkind, in blond wig and white dress, being the demure, loyal Micaëla; Beatrice Gordon, with charcoal mustache, strutting as Don José; and, of course, a vibrant female chorus in the garb of old Jewish men, looking not unlike some members of the audience. But if it is nothing else, Jewish humor is self-depreciatory, and everybody had a wonderful time. "We were a smash," Lenny has said. "Even Sam loved it. He lent us his wigs, after all. It was the sort of innocent musical fun he approved of for me—good relaxation but not a career." And it was a sort of Jewish Andy Hardy movie come to life, with Lenny as Mickey Rooney ("Say, gang, why don't we put on our *own* show, right here in Sharon!").

Two summers later, Lenny and his friends were confident enough to produce a far more ambitious effort. They called themselves the Sharon Community Players, and they put on Gilbert and Sullivan's "The Mikado," almost in its entirety, at the Sharon Town Hall auditorium. The admission price was a dollar, the proceeds going for the hall rental, seventy-five-cent honorarium to each performer, and the balance to charity. Lenny once again assigned the leading role, Nanki-Poo, to himself (there was no inversion of the sexes, the joke having paled since the Carmen production), and, because he had hammered the words and music into his sister's eleven-year-old head during the previous winter, he gave the female lead, Yum-Yum, to Shirley, a seasoned amateur by that summer of 1935. Some semi-professionals were involved, ringers from a local family of piano teachers and singers named Bock. For one antic month, daily rehearsals took place in our Sharon living room, around a tinny upright, with the two dozen or so mostly adolescent cast members unspringing sofas and chairs, raiding the family icebox, and, after the ice-cream truck had tinkled its presence outside, leaving Hoodsie cups and Fudgsicle sticks all over the furniture and floors. My mother's patience, limitless the previous summer, was in danger of running out. The daily din, the unrepressed energy of youth, the picking up after sloppy teen-agers took their toll on her, but she was secretly proud. My father simply removed himself to quieter quarters whenever he could, reserving his indignant rages for weekends. "It's *Shabbas!*" he'd shout at Lenny. "Stop playing the piano and go to *shul!*" I was just a toddling three-year-old, but I remember enjoying the frenetic scene in my house. I have been told that I learned by rote practically the entire the score of "The Mikado," while I was supposed to be having my afternoon naps.

The niece of Morris Finn, who later sent me a letter about my first Grove story, participated in "The Mikado." About that event, she wrote me, "We had such fun rehearsing, and when we came to the song 'I've Got a Little List,' Lenny insisted on holding a roll of toilet tissue and reading from it. It sounds silly now, but it still makes me laugh. The night of the great performance saw me in the hospital with a sudden appendectomy, and I was bitterly disappointed. But during my convalescence at the home of Beatrice Gordon, my cousin, in Roxbury, Lenny came over, and sitting at the piano, played and sang the entire score of 'The Mikado,' and acted out each part. He was wonderful. With all the concerts I've seen him do on TV since, I have never got a greater bang out of anything than that impromptu performance. . . ."

"The Mikado" was such a roaring success that the next summer Lenny, soon to be a cocky Harvard sophomore, decided to produce "H.M.S Pinafore"—the complete Gilbert and Sullivan opus, with a Bernstein-choreographed addition of an "Aida" ballet. "At the time of 'Pinafore,' I had fallen in love with 'Aida,' particularly with the ballet music," Lenny has since explained. "I was determined to get it into 'Pinafore' somehow, and so when Sir Joseph Porter is welcomed aboard the ship by Captain Corcoran I blithely added a line for Captain Corcoran to say, by way of entertaining his guest—'Bring on the Egyptian dancing girls!' At which point Shirley and the Kaplan twins, Jean and Thelma, clad in cheesecloth belly-dancer costumes, appeared as an Egyptian princess and her handmaidens, wriggling to a bit of Verdi's ballet music. It was all very arbitrary and over in a few minutes. Then we just went on with 'Pinafore.' "

Lenny's voice had lowered to baritone, preventing him from snatching the tenor lead, Ralph Rackstraw (that role was sung by young Victor Alpert, who went on to become the librarian of the Boston Symphony Orchestra); instead, Lenny sang the baritone part of Captain Corcoran, thus enabling him to deliver that startling line "Bring on the Egyptian dancing girls!" But the show-stopping discovery of the production was our new maid, Lelia Jiampietro, who was commandeered by Lenny to play Josephine, the Captain's daughter. Lelia was hired at the beginning of the summer to replace another maid who, it emerged, had contracted gonorrhea. (After her disease was confirmed by our family physician, "Dr. Finky," and she was summarily dismissed, my mother and father, like possessed chars, scrubbed the entire house with Lysol and Sea Breeze. It was the finest hour in Sam's lifelong battle with germs. For days, the place smelled like a hospital ward.) Lenny had immediately noticed that the new maid sang to herself in a sweet, pure voice while she washed the dishes and swept the floors. He insisted to Jennie that Lelia was born to play Josephine, and, to everybody's amazement, my mother agreed. Perhaps she was softened by the knowledge that rehearsals would take place at the Town Hall, not in our living room. Lenny also commandeered Jennie's Plymouth Roadster, which my father had bought for his wife's exclusive use. But the Plymouth was a larky means of transporting the players to rehearsals. So Jennie would stand each morning by the kitchen door, mop in hand, not quite believing the sight that greeted her eyes: at least ten kids in *her* car driving off with *her* maid for the day. Lenny was one hell of a persuader. He could talk his mother into sailing the Atlantic in a catboat, if he set his mind to it.

He even made some headway with his father. Without

serious complaint, Sam allowed Lenny to major in music at Harvard, although he dearly hoped that Lenny would concentrate on something practical, like economics. Sam still balked at subsidizing advanced piano lessons with Heinrich Gebhard, but Lenny had enough students of his own and pickup-band gigs to cover that expense. While Gebhard enlarged his talented pupil's repertoire and musical perception, Harvard broadened Lenny's intellectual and political interests. He was exposed to the puzzles of history, philosophy, and literature, and to the passions of left-wing politics, the Spanish Civil War being in full fury. But music was his primary concern. He studied composition and theory with such distinguished academicians as Walter Piston, Arthur Tillman Merritt, and Edward Burlingame Hill, and he plunged into the active Cambridge musical scene. He was a pianist for the Glee Club, for less formal student events that required a musician with a sense of fun, and even for silent movies offered by the university's film society. (During one screening of "The Battleship Potemkin," he accompanied the film with bits of Copland's arcane "Piano Variations," Stravinsky's "Petrouchka," and some Russian-Jewish folk tunes he had learned from Sam.) He also wrote smart-alecky, sophomoric reviews of concerts by Serge Koussevitzky (whom he had yet to meet) and the Boston Symphony Orchestra, and he appeared as the soloist in the Ravel Piano Concerto with the State Symphony Orchestra, an organization financed by the Works Progress Administration.

In 1939, toward the end of his senior year, Lenny wrote the incidental music for the Harvard Classical Club's production, in the original Greek, of Aristophanes' "The Birds," parts of that score later surfacing in "On the Town." And he conducted the small orchestra, marking his first appearance on a podium. When the Harvard Student Union defied the Boston authorities and presented a bare-stage performance of Marc Blitzstein's proletarian opera "The Cradle Will Rock," Lenny was selected to direct and play the piano for the ambitious effort, at Sanders Theatre. Again, he called on his sister, by then fifteen and a junior at Newton High School, to sing a role—browbeating Shirley into believing that she could handle the part, and sweet-talking Jennie and Sam into permitting it. It took a lot of sweet-talking, because the part she sang was that of Moll, a down-and-out prostitute, but Lenny was still a grand persuader. Shirley sang the role beautifully, assuming the name, in the program, of Shirley Mann; the audience thought she was a Radcliffe student. If Jennie and Sam experienced mixed feelings at the performance, everybody else was exhilarated. The Harvard community and the Boston critics were stunned by the professionalism and power of the student production. (Shirley Mann was singled out for special praise.) Marc Blitzstein, who had come to Cambridge to see his opera, was quoted as saying that Lenny, playing the piano for the singers, "did it better than I did" at the famous Orson Welles-John Houseman New York production, in 1937. The mutual admiration of Blitzstein and Bernstein developed into a firm friendship, lasting until Blitzstein's tragic death, in 1964. The musical influences each had on the other were telling for both them and future theatre audiences.

Two other professional friendships begun at Harvard were even more telling. When Lenny was still an undergraduate, he met Aaron Copland and Dimitri Mitropoulos. Copland, who was then well on his way to earning the title "Dean of American Composers," had influenced Lenny long before they were introduced. Lenny had mastered Copland's "Piano Variations" and had been taken with the distinctly American style of his other works. At their first meeting, Copland recognized Lenny's talent and suggested that he think about becoming a composer. And Mitropoulos, who was appearing as a guest conductor with the Boston Symphony, turned Lenny's head in yet another musical direction. Their friendship came about as a fluke —a touch of fate innocently initiated by, of all people, Jennie.

Lenny had received a rather casual invitation to attend a Sunday reception for Mitropoulos given by the Harvard Helicon Society at Phillips Brooks House, but he had planned to spend most of that Sunday at home in Newton. When it came time for him to return to his room, at Eliot House, Jennie offered to drive him back to Cambridge. She put a coat on over her plain housedress, and they set out in her Plymouth Roadster. Jennie's automotive habits were every bit as infuriating as Sam's. She tended to sing and play the radio while she drove, keeping time to the music by tapping the accelerator. Beyond the damage that that odd practice did to the automobile, it unnerved her passengers, caused several minor accidents over the years, and often so distracted her from the matter at hand that she became lost, even in familiar territory. Such was the case that fateful Sunday afternoon. Instead of pulling up in front of Eliot House, she missed a crucial turn and ended up in front of Phillips Brooks House. Lenny suddenly remembered the reception for Mitropoulos and badgered Jennie into dropping in on the party with him, despite her protestations about her inappropriate clothing. Clutching her coat about her housedress, she entered the crowded reception room with Lenny, and they stood in line to meet the visiting maestro. After the introductions, Mitropoulos, who had been told by some other guests that Lenny was an outstanding undergraduate musician, asked Lenny to play something for him, and he did, with the unalloyed chutzpah of his youth and his adulthood. As Jennie looked on with a mixture of astonishment and pride, her son performed a Chopin nocturne and a movement of a piano sonata he had composed.

Mitropoulos was impressed enough to invite Lenny to attend his rehearsals that week at Symphony Hall. Witness-

ing at first hand the strength and musicianship of Mitropoulos at work with the virtuosic Boston Symphony, Lenny
was overwhelmed. The idea of becoming a conductor himself was far too remote to be anything more than a glim-
mering possibility, but that dim vision was nevertheless
perceptible. Later, Mitropoulos took Lenny to an oyster
lunch, called him a "genius boy," and made that glimmer-
ing possibility seem brighter still by suggesting a sym-
phony-conducting career for him. Both composition and
conducting had been recommended by men of lofty professional standing, and young Lenny—whose commitment to
the narrow discipline of being a concert pianist was perhaps
waning—took them seriously.

*T*HE FOUR-YEAR PERIOD FOL-
lowing Lenny's graduation from Harvard, in June of 1939,
was an erratic high dive culminating in the splendid splash
of his unexpected début with the New York Philharmonic.
With Lenny leaning toward the even more esoteric and
unrewarding musical fields of composition and conducting, Sam was doubly dubious. The world was on the verge
of cataclysm; the safest place for a college graduate—no
matter what his demonstrated artistic gifts—was in the security of the family business. But Sam allowed Lenny to
have one last fling, a summer in New York City. He reasoned that once Lenny had seen for himself the unhappy
lot of the musician in the big time he would return to
Boston and gratefully accept an executive position in the
Samuel Bernstein Hair Company. To insure this outcome,
he gave Lenny barely enough money to last the summer.

The first person Lenny got in touch with in New York
was Adolph Green, who was then one-fifth of a struggling
night-club act called the Revuers. (The other members of

that pioneer group of sophisticated satirists were Betty Comden, Judy Holliday, Alvin Hammer, and John Frank.) Green offered Lenny a bed in his Greenwich Village apartment and an occasional chance to play the piano for the Revuers at the Village Vanguard, where they entertained a limited but loyal coterie. And when they were asked to record one of their longer sketches, an insane Hollywood saga called "The Girl with the Two Left Feet," Lenny earned twenty-five dollars as their accompanist. As for other musicianly work, there was none—especially if one wasn't in the union, and membership in Local 802 of the American Federation of Musicians required a six-month residency in New York. Still, Lenny had fun. He was among people in show business and music, and the people seemed to respect his talents. He had tasted the city and found it to his liking. Then the summer and the money ran out. As a last musical gesture, he bought a clarinet in a pawnshop (a balky instrument with a cracked bell, which later fell into my inept hands), and he glumly returned to Boston.

Before total resignation to his imminent business career set in, however, Lenny heard from a friend that Mitropoulos was in New York and would like to see the "genius boy." Lenny made a quick trip back to New York. At their meeting, Mitropoulos insisted that Lenny should commit himself to music, specifically to conducting, and he suggested that Lenny enter the Curtis Institute, in Philadelphia, where he could study with the great Fritz Reiner, director of the Pittsburgh Symphony Orchestra. Although the academic year was about to begin, Mitropoulos said he could arrange an audition with Reiner. The audition was successful, and Lenny was immediately accepted at Curtis, with the attendant scholarship. Calling forth his ultimate powers of persuasion, he gained Sam's reluctant blessing and some expense money. For two years, he studied conducting with Reiner, orchestration with Randall Thompson, and piano with Isabelle Vengerova—all of them uncompromising masters, accustomed to teaching prodigies with few interests outside music. It was a strange milieu for a worldy Harvard graduate, but he learned—had to learn—discipline and technique. He excelled, not always happily.

Of equal professional importance were the next two summers. Serge Koussevitzky and the Boston Symphony had been presenting concerts for several summers at Tanglewood, an estate in the Berkshires bequeathed to the orchestra, and in 1940 Koussevitzky inaugurated the Berkshire Music Center as an adjunct to Tanglewood. According to his plan, worthy young musicians of various disciplines would study with a distinguished faculty in pleasant natural surroundings; student conductors—an élite few, supervised by Koussevitzky himself—would actually practice their skills with a full-size student orchestra. Thanks to strong letters of recommendation, Lenny was chosen as one of three student conductors in the inaugural year. Falling under the spell of Koussevitzky (whose expressive nineteenth-century manner affected even the groundskeepers of Tanglewood), Lenny was soaring from the start, as a letter home, written soon after his arrival there, indicates:

DEAREST FOLKS—

. . . I have never seen such a beautiful setup in my life. I've been conducting the orchestra every morning, & I'm playing my first concert tomorrow night. Kouss gave me the hardest & longest number of all—the Second Symphony of Randall Thompson. 30 minutes long—a modern American work—as my first performance. And Kouss is so pleased with my work. He likes me & works very hard with me in our private sessions. He is the most marvelous man—a beautiful spirit that never lags or fails—that inspires me terrifically. And he told me he is convinced that I have a wonderful gift, & he is already making me a *great* conductor. (I actually rode in his car with him today!) He has won-

derful teaching ability, which I never expected—& is very hard
to please—so that when he says he is pleased I know it means
something. I am so thrilled—have never been more happy &
satisfied. The orchestra likes me very much, best of all the conductors, & responds so beautifully in rehearsal. Of course, the
concert tomorrow night (Shabbas, yet!) will tell whether I can
keep my head in performance. We've been working very hard—
you're always going like mad here—no time to think of how tired
you are or how little you slept last night—the inspiration of this
Center is terrific enough to keep you going with no sleep at all.
I'm so excited about tomorrow night—I wish you could all be
here—it's so important to me—& Kouss is banking on it to convince him that he's right—if it goes well there's no telling what
may happen . . .

Please come up—I think I'll be conducting every Friday night
& rehearsing every morning—please come up—

All my love—
LENNY

Jennie was beside herself with pleasure, and even Sam
couldn't help feeling stirrings of pride in his son, the apparent favorite of Koussevitzky. But who was this Koussevitzky, so rapidly becoming another father to Lenny,
usurping Sam's rightful place? Sam knew that Koussevitzky, like him, had been born a Russian Jew, but, unlike
Sam, had converted to Christianity in order to further his
musical career in the motherland. What kind of man was
this, who would do such a thing? And would he try to
convert Lenny in order to further his career? (Sam didn't
know it then, but Koussevitzky was already hinting to his
Lenyushka that Leonard S. Burns would be a more pre-
sentable name for a conductor, the "S" being for Samuel-
ovich. Lenny thought about it for a while and then put the
idea out of his mind.) Sam needn't have worried about his
son's Jewishness, which was so irrevocably a part of him
that even Koussevitzky had no influence on it. Indeed, just

the previous year Lenny had begun to compose a piece for soprano and orchestra based on the Book of Lamentations, and it was dedicated to "my father." There was *nachas* for you! But still Sam felt jealous, indignant, and, worst of all, impotent. Lenny was being lost to him, and there wasn't much he could do about it—except control the purse strings. When Sam finally drove Jennie, Shirley, and me to Tanglewood from Sharon, it was obvious that everything Lenny had said in his letter was true. The place seemed to have been invented for him alone.

There followed another rigorous year at Curtis and another glorious summer at Tanglewood, at which Lenny was clearly recognized as *the* protégé of Koussevitzky—perhaps someday, it was rumored, the heir, if the board of trustees of the Boston Symphony could ever defy tradition and appoint a young American as conductor. It was only a fantasy rumor, not to be seriously discussed. And with the draft, Lenny's career would likely take a military turn. However, at his first Army physical he was classified 4-F because of chronic asthma. (The Army doctor who thus deferred him happened to be a celebrated asthma specialist.) It was humiliating and frustrating for Lenny not to be in uniform while just about everybody else was preparing for war, but there was nothing to be done.

In the fall of 1941, he was a twenty-three-year-old trained and promising musician with no place to go. He returned to Boston, where the gray presence of the Samuel Bernstein Hair Company hung heavily in the air. Koussevitzky tried his best to help. He arranged to have Lenny play as soloist in the Boston Symphony's première of a piano concerto by Carlos Chávez, but union problems cancelled the performance. In desperation, Lenny wangled enough money out of Sam to rent a drafty studio on Huntington Avenue, and he sent out announcements that he was available as a piano teacher. Sam assumed that this venture would fail—making Lenny a candidate once again for his business, just a couple of miles away—and Sam was right. Lenny's studio came into formal existence just two days before Pearl Harbor was attacked, and piano lessons were not top public priority that week. He was rejected by the military, by piano students, and, it seemed, by the entire world. He worked on his compositions (a clarinet sonata and the Lamentations piece), played a few minor-league concerts, and took some encouragement from his close relationship with Koussevitzky. One notable bright spot during the dreary winter was the appearance of Adolph Green and Betty Comden as performers in "My Dear Public," a calamitous musical by the composer-lyricist Irving Caesar, which was trying out in Boston. It was the first professional theater I had ever seen, and it baffled my ten-year-old mind no less than it did the adult audience's. I can safely say that from its opening number to its finale, nobody knew for sure what was happening on stage. (Irving Caesar was also the author of the enigmatic words for the song "Tea for Two.")

The summer of 1942 brought some cheer. Lenny returned to Tanglewood (its last full season for the duration) not as a student but as the assistant to Koussevitzky, with teaching responsibilities. But when the summer ended he was back in the bind. Reopening the Huntington Avenue studio would be flirting with fiscal and emotional disaster, so he tried New York again, a last stab at the big time. New York was even grimmer than Boston. It marked a period that Lenny has referred to as "my Valley Forge." From a cheap furnished room, he went forth looking for work, any work. What he found was the occasional odd job: vocal coach, rehearsal pianist, dollar-an-hour piano teacher, and —to contribute to the war effort—performer for the soldiers at Fort Dix, New Jersey. Through the auspices of Irving Caesar, he landed a steady twenty-five-dollar-a-week position with a music publisher, transcribing jazz improvisations, arranging songs for piano, and writing original pop tunes, under the name "Lenny Amber." That job at least rescued him from the ultimate defeat of returning to Boston and Sam's business. He had some money to live on and some time to compose. His piece for soprano and orchestra, based on the Book of Lamentations, had developed into the "Jeremiah Symphony." He entered it in a competition for American music which was sponsored by the New England Conservatory, but it didn't win the prize, and, worse yet, Koussevitzky didn't think much of it. But it won some points with Sam, who relished its Jewish thematic material and its dedication to him.

Although there was no formal Tanglewood season the following summer, Koussevitzky was spending the warm months at his estate, Seranak, overlooking the Tanglewood grounds. He invited Lenny to visit and help him with a benefit there for the Red Cross. Lenny, his prospects apparently no brighter, arrived at Seranak on the day before his twenty-fifth birthday and was informed by Koussevitzky that Artur Rodzinski, the recently appointed music director of the New York Philharmonic, wished to see him. Rodzinski owned a farm in nearby Stockbridge, where Lenny met the conductor on his birthday morning. They chatted amiably in an asthma-inducing hayfield, while the wheezing Lenny wondered why he had been summoned. At last, it was made clear. Rodzinski abruptly declared that he had seen Lenny conduct the Tanglewood student orchestra the summer before, and he had since come to believe that Lenny would be right for the post of assistant conductor of the New York Philharmonic. Besides, said Rodzinski, who was a confirmed Buchmanite and claimed to communicate directly with the Lord, God had told him to "take Bernstein." One did not argue with divine intervention. Lenny became the assistant conductor of the Philharmonic, without so much as an audition before a professional orchestra. It was one hell of a birthday present.

The Kids

*A*FTER THE SHOCK OF THIS momentous news had worn off, it turned out to be somewhat less momentous. The position of assistant conductor meant, in actuality, being little more than a white-collar flunky for the maestro: checking acoustic levels in Carnegie Hall, attending all rehearsals, studying the scores for the week's concerts, and sometimes running small errands. Of course, in an extreme emergency the assistant had to be prepared to take over the baton, although established conductors had a notorious reputation for reaching the podium with the aid of crutches, if need be. But the assistant received a decent salary (enabling Lenny to rent a studio apartment in the Carnegie Hall building), and his name appeared in the program every week. Prestige and the vague possibility of conducting someday were fringe benefits of the job. Once, when Sam and Jennie asked Lenny if he would ever get a chance to conduct the Philharmonic, he told them, in effect, not to hold their breath. For Jennie, it didn't really matter; her son had already fulfilled most of her expectations. For Sam, it meant that, while Lenny seemed to be lost to him and his business, there was still some faint hope of his coming home to Boston if Lenny grew weary enough of his chores. This hope, however, became fainter when Lenny excitedly informed them that Fritz Reiner had invited him to Pittsburgh to conduct the world première of the "Jeremiah Symphony" in January of 1944, and that Koussevitzky had asked Lenny to conduct the same work with the Boston Symphony later that winter. And of more immediate importance was the performance of Lenny's latest composition—"I Hate Music," a cycle of five "kid songs"—by the mezzo-soprano Jennie Tourel, who was making her New York recital début at Town Hall on Saturday night, November 13, 1943.

Such was the consequence of the Jennie Tourel recital that Lenny demanded the family's presence. My parents and I were living full time in Sharon then, the Newton house having been sold. With my father's customary striving for flawless planning on any sort of trip—tantamount, in my eyes, to an invasion of a Pacific atoll by the Marines —Sam drove Jennie and me from Sharon to Back Bay Station fully two hours earlier than the train to New York was scheduled to depart, on that slushy November Saturday. (Shirley was away at college and couldn't spare the time for the trip.) To kill the two hours of waiting, I explored the musty recesses of Back Bay Station while Sam fretfully studied his watch and Jennie read the local Hearst paper. Late that afternoon, we arrived in New York and checked into the Barbizon-Plaza Hotel, Sam's new stopping place since he had met with some affront at the Hotel New Yorker. He rushed us through dinner so that we would be at Town Hall at least an hour before the recital began and half an hour before Lenny was supposed to meet us at the box office with our tickets.

Even with the exhilaration the evening promised—Lenny's first hearing as a composer before a sophisticated New York audience—my brother seemed unusually atremble when he met us in the lobby. What he didn't dare disclose was that the Philharmonic's associate manager, Bruno Zirato, had informed him of some terrifying news earlier in the day: Bruno Walter, the guest conductor of the Philharmonic that week, had been taken ill with influenza. He had a fever and his stomach was upset. It was possible, remotely possible, that Maestro Walter would not be in condition to conduct the rather exacting program on Sunday afternoon, which was to be broadcast throughout America by CBS. If such a dire situation did arise, and Rodzinski wasn't able to drive through the snow from his Stockbridge farm to substitute for Walter, then Lenny would have to step in. It was all very unlikely but very frightening, in a B-movie sort of way. To be on the safe side, Zirato told Lenny to study Walter's scores for the program—Schumann's Overture to "Manfred," Miklós Rózsa's "Theme, Variations, and Finale," Strauss's "Don Quixote," and Wagner's Prelude to "Die Meistersinger."

The Tourel recital went beautifully, and the reception given to Lenny's cycle of "kid songs"—an amusing audience pleaser—was, as I recall, tittering and warm, like encore appreciations of "Short'nin' Bread." (I recall not much more of the recital. I was one of those eleven-year-old philistines who are determined to ignore concert music, especially recital music, and I had to be nudged to attention by my mother for the performance of Lenny's piece.) After the concert, Sam whisked Jennie and me back to the hotel, although Jennie very much wanted to go on to a party with Lenny at the singer's apartment. I think that Sam was confused by the acclaim his son had received for such a short and, to him, incomprehensible work. Anyway, he felt uncomfortable among all those "artist people." He used my age and heavy eyelids as sound reasons for our returning forthwith to the Barbizon-Plaza. But Lenny, shining with his success and barely able to keep the report of Walter's illness to himself, went on to the celebration. Ordinarily, he is the last to leave a party, and that evening, despite the beckoning of those Walter scores and all they potentially represented, was no exception. But he was well acquainted with the program from his previous studying of the scores and Walter's rehearsals and concerts earlier that week. As dawn broke over New York, he left the Tourel party and returned to his apartment for some fitful sleep. He was awakened at nine o'clock by a phone call from Zirato. Maestro Walter was too sick to perform that afternoon, Zirato told him, and Rodzinski would not have enough time to drive down from Stockbridge to make the three-o'clock concert. "You're going to conduct," Zirato said.

According to Sam's meticulous itinerary, we were to take the one-o'clock train back to Boston after having lunched at the hotel's coffee shop and strolled through Central Park. (Now that I think of it, how odd that Sam never showed his family the crumbling landmarks of his first years in New York! Perhaps he was embarrassed, although he certainly enjoyed talking about his toil at the Fulton Fish Market, for instance.) Just before we left our room, Lenny phoned and said, in the voice of an ingenuous adolescent, that we should cancel our plans to return to Boston, that we should book the hotel room for another night, and that we should pick up three tickets at the Carnegie Hall box office for seats in the conductor's box—because he, Lenny Bernstein, son and brother to his family, was going to conduct the Philharmonic that very afternoon. "*Oy, gevalt!*" I remember my parents saying, almost in unison, both of them holding their cheeks, as if to prevent their faces from collapsing. Quickly, Lenny went on to explain what had happened, what had brought about this incredible turn of events. He said that there had been no time for a rehearsal but that he had visited Bruno Walter at his hotel and consulted with him about the scores for the program, although Walter was shivering and feverish. Lenny described himself as hardly better off, exhausted from lack of sleep and in a state of near-shock. "Wish me luck," he said. "And come backstage at intermission."

My memories of the rest of that day are these: Sam and Jennie, color absent from their faces, forgot about lunch in the coffee shop downstairs. After telephone calls to Shirley, at Mount Holyoke, and some special friends—telling them all repeatedly that they could *hear* the concert on the *radio*—they headed directly to Carnegie Hall, a block down Seventh Avenue from the hotel. Sam was by no means going to be late for his son's première; indeed, he was about three hours early. As Lenny had said, the tickets for the conductor's box were waiting for us. It was true—Lenny was the conductor. With so much time to kill, we went back to the hotel. My parents tried to rest while I prowled the lobby, buying Charleston Chews at the candy counter and wolfing them down with the abandon of sudden, unexpected adult freedom.

At two o'clock, we were back in Carnegie Hall, being led to the conductor's box by an usher. The majesty and the immensity of the place stunned me, especially in comparison with Town Hall. As the audience filed in, it dawned on me that they were all coming to see my brother, whether they knew it then or not. Sam and Jennie sat in their seats as decorously as possible, given their unease, my mother whispering warnings about my leaning over the box's velvety railing. I heard my father sigh when he spotted some photographers, who had obviously been tipped off to an impending news event, wandering about the corridor with their Graflexes. At last, the hall was filled—more people, it seemed from my perspective, than I had ever imagined could fit in one enclosed space—and the orchestra, cacophonously tuning, was settled onstage. Then, an enormous, bearlike man walked out of the wings to the podium, and an awful silence fell. Bruno Zirato announced to the assembled, in a low voice colored with a gruff Italian accent, that Maestro Walter was ill but that we were all going "to witness the début of a full-fledged conductor who was born, educated, and trained in this country." He meant my brother. A few people left the hall, and I stared at them in anger. It wasn't fair. He hadn't even started to conduct yet. Then Lenny came out onstage, wearing a gray suit and looking much younger and less elegant than the orchestra musicians. He sort of hopped onto the podium. I didn't know whether it was proper for me to join in the wavelet of applause; it had died away by the time I had decided to contribute a clap or two. I could feel myself blushing. Sam sighed again, Jennie gripped my knee, Lenny raised and brought down his arms, and the concert began.

I don't remember much about the music itself except that it sounded all right to me and that Lenny seemed to know what he was doing. The Overture to "Manfred" was loud (the way I liked concert music best), and so was the applause afterward. The Miklós Rózsa piece, which was forgettable, was less heartily received. Lenny took several bows, and the lights grew brighter. Somebody from the Philharmonic staff, who was also sitting in the box, led us through a pressing crowd of well-wishers, reporters, and photographers to the greenroom backstage, where Lenny was talking to a lot of important-looking people. He was perspiring, and he seemed much thinner than he had the night before—hollow-eyed, like war refugees in news photos. His smile was so broad that it covered his whole face. He embraced Sam and Jennie, whose eyes were glazed with wonder and emotion. When he saw me, he ruffled my hair and gave me a big hug and a kiss. He said, "Hey, kid, how did it go?" I was too shy in front of all those people to answer with more than a mumble, but I was proud. Somebody said that Rodzinski had just arrived from Stockbridge, and the greenroom was cleared. Lenny kissed us all again, and we went back to the box. Some of the reporters in the corridor realized that Sam and Jennie were the conductor's parents, but the Philharmonic man kept them away.

When Lenny came out onstage again, the applause was very loud. Two soloists joined him for Strauss's "Don Quixote"—a cellist, Joseph Schuster, and a violist, William Lincer. Really big applause after that piece. But when Lenny conducted Wagner's "Die Meistersinger" (whose grand themes I knew by heart from Lenny's banging them out on the piano at home) and the concert ended, the house roared like one giant animal in a zoo. It was certainly the loudest human sound I had ever heard—thrilling and eerie. People were shouting at Lenny and the orchestra. Some of them moved toward the front of the stage. We all stood up and applauded with them, without thinking about whether we should or not. Again and again, Lenny came out to bow, looking skinnier each time but always flashing that amazing smile. Once, he waved to us in the box, and everybody stared.

Finally, it was over. All the people were talking at once. Lenny had done it, they said—a rugged program, but he had carried it off as if he had been doing it for years. The crush in the greenroom was terrible. A path was cleared for us to Lenny, and there was a lot more hugging and kissing, even crying. The reporters cornered Sam and Jennie, whose faces were now flushed and radiant. While Jennie just repeated, "I'm very proud of him," Sam found his tongue and held forth for the press. "Just the other day," declared Sam, "I said to Lenny, 'If you could only conduct the "Don Quixote"!' And he said, 'Dad, you'll have to wait ten years for that,' " It was mostly fantasy, of course; Sam had never heard of "Don Quixote" before that afternoon. A reporter approached me and asked my age and full name. I lied about my age, saying I was already twelve (an exaggeration of two and a half months), and then I added, "I'd rather you called me Burtie if I'm going to be in the paper." That deathless line went out over the Associated Press wire and was, for some reason, published throughout the nation.

It appeared that everybody in New York City wanted to photograph, interview, or simply be near Lenny—and, failing that, his parents—both in Carnegie Hall and later at a noisy dinner celebration. The next morning, the *Times* and the *Herald Tribune* carried lengthy front-page stories about the event, and the critics were unanimous in their praise of Lenny's vigor, youth, musical gifts, and poise. Even the *News* saw the profound human element in an area generally beyond its coverage, comparing Lenny's last-minute substitution for Walter to "a shoestring catch in center field." ("Make it and you're a hero," the *News* reporter wrote. "Muff it and you're a dope. . . . He made it.") The press strained to find similar situations in musical history. By a remarkable coincidence, Rodzinski had first conducted a major orchestra in 1926 when he took over the performance of "Don Quixote" on short notice from an indisposed Leopold Stokowski. And in 1886, at the Rio de Janeiro opera house, a young cellist named Arturo Toscanini had been called upon to lead the orchestra in an emergency. They were Europeans, however, and the world expected promising young conductors to be Europeans. The irresistible fascination and drama of Lenny's story was that, as Zirato had said before the concert, he was "a full-fledged conductor who was born, educated, and trained in this country." The impossible had happened. A twenty-five-year-old American kid had made it big in a profession that had previously had no room for American kids. The *Times* said in an editorial, "It's a good American success story. The warm, friendly triumph of it filled Carnegie Hall and spread far over the airwaves." Lenny possessed talent, ambition, and luck. They all miraculously came together to make him famous overnight. Before long, he would be one of the most celebrated men in the world. It was just like in the movies.

And the whole family was suddenly a cast of characters in a movie. We were thrust willy-nilly into the public eye, objects of curiosity not only to our acquaintances but also to people we had never heard of. Dazzled and confused, Jennie and Sam were beset by interviewers and instant new friends and advisers. Strangers, assuming the right of intimacy, would ask, "How does it feel to be the parents of a genius? How did you do it?" Some would counsel, "Tell your son he shouldn't go to Hollywood," while others said, "Lenny should be in movies, he's so handsome—a natural showman." A few instant enemies also emerged and spread the rumors that Lenny was going to change his religion and that Sam had bribed Bruno Walter to feign illness so Lenny could have his chance to conduct the Philharmonic. Those rumors were so patently absurd that they hardly bothered my parents; still, they kept cropping up.

Beauty-salon owners began to place their orders directly with Sam rather than through his salesmen, just so they could have a talk with him in his office about his wonderful son. (The salesmen complained, but they were pleased with their celebrity association nevertheless.) The Boston Jewish community, in particular, adopted Lenny as a collective son—he was Boston's own, and a Jewish boy, after all—and people of my parents' generation absorbed vicarious *nachas* by merely being in the same room as Jennie and Sam. Everybody, it seemed, had heard about Lenny's incredible début and the successes that followed in rapid order. Everybody had known him when. Everybody called him "Lenny." The man who delivered the fuel oil in Sharon had read all about it. So had my homeroom teacher, Miss Henderson. Distant cousins—some so distant as to be totally unknown—sent clippings and warm expressions of familial cheer.

Lenny's fame triggered a new optimism for the family. Shirley had almost finished college, and the business was flourishing again as beauty supplies became more plentiful once the Allies had definitely taken the road to victory. Glowing with the brighter outlook, Sam bought a "winter house" in Brookline early in 1944, keeping the Sharon house for summers and weekends, once again. Our new neighborhood in Brookline was all abuzz with the news that Lenny Bernstein's family was moving in. Sam was the most dazzled and confused by Lenny's fame and the attention being paid to him and his family. After all, it was he who had made no secret of his unhappiness with Lenny's artistic bent. Indeed, he had used his considerable power to obstruct it. Could he now take credit, in part, for the miracle? At first, he tried. In his initial interviews with the hungry press, his statements were of the "I knew-he-had-it-in-him-all-the-time" variety. One multicolumn interview, with photographs, on the feature page of the Boston Sunday *Post* prompted general wincing. Its headline read:

FATHER IN TEARS AT BOY
CONDUCTOR'S TRIUMPH
BOSTON MERCHANT CALLS SON'S
ACCOMPLISHMENT,
"MY CONTRIBUTION TO AN AMERICA
THAT HAS DONE
EVERYTHING FOR ME"

The article went on to state such embarrassments as "Papa Bernstein spent over $12,000 for Lennie's [the *Post's* spelling] education, but it was worth it."

However, Lenny was giving out many more interviews, and he, too, was inexperienced in dealing with the press. He was uncommonly frank about his father, describing Sam as something of an ogre, who had done all he could to prevent Lenny from being a musician. Sam, who subscribed to a clipping service for a while and kept a scrapbook of pieces about Lenny, saw these statements and was hurt, although he knew they were basically true. Once, when he was questioned by a reporter about this ogreism, he replied, "From the early sixteenth century, my family never made a livelihood in art, and I didn't want to break this tradition. I also felt Lenny could make a better living in business. Remember, there was no Leonard Bernstein then. . . . I'm very proud of Lenny, but the Talmud teaches us, 'Don't expect miracles.' . . . If I had to do it all over again, I'd do the same thing." Sam made a good point: If a Leonard Bernstein had never existed before, how could you know that your talented kid would grow up to be a Leonard Bernstein? There was no such thing as a young, famous, respected American conductor before Lenny emerged on that November Sunday afternoon. Today, any accomplished American youngster can, theoretically, become a conductor, but Lenny was the fellow who set the precedent. Perhaps Sam could be faulted for a lack of faith in his gifted son, but not for a lack of prescience. He wanted only the best for Lenny, and the best meant a secure, comfortable life. For years after Lenny's initial success, Sam harbored doubts about the stability of his son's career. He worried that it would somehow all come tumbling down, like a construction made of Pick-Up Sticks. When he confided these needless worries to me, I suspected that he still secretly wished that Lenny would one day return to Boston and the beauty-supplies business. Then, triumphantly, Sam's ogreism would be vindicated.

It was the nature of my father to worry, even when things were going far better than he had ever dared to hope. If there was absolutely nothing to fret about, he would invent something. Instead of forgetting the past and enjoying the present, he preferred to stew—perhaps from guilt, perhaps from a feeling of not being appreciated. His morose silences and depressions returned, this time accompanied by ulcers. When he first experienced the symptoms (stomach pains, after, say, a bountiful *kiddush*, and lingering nausea—"varming" was his neologism for it), he chose to ignore them as best he could. But the symptoms grew worse, and he consulted a specialist, "a famous stomach man at Beth Israel Hospital." The stomach man put him on a strict diet and told him not to worry so much. The former instruction Sam more or less obeyed; the latter he knew was impossible. If he neglected his bland, lactic diet (while entertaining a business associate at Locke-Ober's, for instance), he would manage to blame others for his failing and the unpleasant consequences. The person who took the brunt of the blame was, of course, his old scapegoat and helpmeet, Jennie. "Jennie," he would cry accusingly from his sickbed, "why did you let me eat that lousy herring, you know the doctor said I'm not supposed to eat herring!" Or, when he knew his wife was within earshot, he would complain loudly, "Jennie served me tea after the ice cream, and I must have told her a thousand times not to serve me tea after the ice cream." It never occurred to him that Jennie could have served him garlic pickles with chocolate sauce but he didn't have to eat them.

As his ulcers and depressions became unbearable—for him and for everybody else—Lenny and Shirley tried to talk him into seeing a psychoanalyst. He declined flatly. But then he developed a painful case of shingles, and he relented. The shingles doctor convinced him that both ulcers and shingles could have psychosomatic origins. (Sam, naturally, pronounced it "psychosemitic.") Willing to grasp any remedy for his miseries, he went off to his first appointment with a Boston psychoanalyst. It was a dark day for Sam—the equivalent of committing himself to a madhouse, as his sister Clara had been committed earlier. But he returned home after that initial consultation in the highest spirits I had witnessed in years. His happy report of that brush with the disciple of Dr. Freud went like this: "He said to me, 'Sit down, Mr. Bernstein, sit down. You don't have to lie on a couch.' So then we sat and talked for a long time about all kinds of things—you know, phil*ah*sephy, good and evil, God, the Talmud. He's a Jewish man, the analyst. And so after we talked the analyst stood up and he shook my hand and he said to me, he said, 'Look, Mr. Bernstein, you should be sitting here where I am and I should be sitting there where you are. You haven't got what you call an inferior complex, or any of those things. If everybody in the world was like you, I'd be out of business. Sitting here listening to you talk, I learned more than I did from all the books. It was a pleasure, believe me. You shouldn't be spending your money and wasting your valuable time talking to me. I should be paying *you*.' And so he tells me I'm all cured, and so I left." There never was a second visit to the psychoanalyst. Months afterward, during a new attack of shingles-cum-depression, Sam was asked if he wanted to have another try with the analyst. "Neh," he replied, "I can get the same advice from my rabbis."

As far as Jennie was concerned, the movie in which we had all suddenly become characters was a shopgirl epic, perhaps starring John Garfield and Joan Crawford—the kind she doted on. There was her brilliant son who, against staggering odds, had made it to the top of his profession. Life, fantastically, had imitated art. And just as she had imagined in her youth, when she read dime novels about the glamorous rich to take her mind off her drudgery in the Lawrence mills, she found herself hobnobbing with those very people in the novels, the famous and wealthy and highborn. Some of them were descendants of the Boston Brahmins who owned those mills, the Yankees who had practiced their golf shots on the lawn outside the mill as the young immigrant Jennie peered at them angrily through a filthy factory window. That was the stuff of a John Garfield-Joan Crawford movie.

These larger-than-life people made a fuss over her. She was the conductor's mother—sweet, homey, winning in her ways, obviously a good parent and wife. She was no stage mother who had pushed and prodded her son into the spotlight. Lenny's admirers were sincerely interested in her. At post-concert social gatherings, she would often rival Lenny himself for attention as imposing men and women sought her out to chat about Lenny's interpretation of a Mahler symphony or her thoughts on the latest exhibition at the Museum of Modern Art. While she never pretended to have any expertise in such arcane matters ("I thought it was very nice, dear," she would most likely answer a question fraught with aesthetic significance), her conversations with the intelligentsia sometimes had memorable results. So amusing were Jennie's often stunning malapropian remarks that her children, with their practiced love of ridicule, began to collect them. We still can hardly wait to share "Jennie stories," and some knowing friends have been dining out on them for decades. I was appointed Keeper of the Jenniana—and, of course, the complementary Samiana.

Through the years, my files of Jenniana and Samiana have thickened. At one point, I entertained the notion of compiling them into a thin volume called "The Jennie Bernstein Cookbook"—so named because of her utter inability to cook, or even to make toast palatable, which flew in the face of the Jewish-mother stereotype. (The aptitude of Jewish mothers to create steaming, succulent meals is rarely questioned.) Indeed, my plan for "The Jennie Bernstein Cookbook" was to begin with her recipe for toast:

1. Awaken, in the manner of J.B., at 6:00 A.M., at least two full hours before anyone else in the house.
2. Remove slices of bread from their wrappers (rye, white, whole wheat, English muffins, or challah may be used, although ordinary white is best for these purposes; old bread of any variety, preserved in the freezer, is preferable).
3. Immediately place bread slices in the toaster, allowing some to be overdone, some underdone.
4. As soon as bread is toasted, liberally butter (and add jam, jelly, honey, etc.).
5. Allow toast to stand until soggy.
6. When the first matutinal stirring of another human is heard, pop the toast into a warm oven for reheating.
7. Announce loudly, "Your toast is ready."
8. Remove pieces of toast from oven, as persons make their way to the breakfast table.
9. Serve only when butter (and/or jam, jelly, honey, etc.) has recongealed and bread is the consistency of moist Kleenex.

The Kids

(Other elements of a normal breakfast may be similarly prepared: grapefruit, orange juice, eggs in any style, coffee. Be sure to prepare a full two hours before served, however.)

Jennie was proud of her breakfasts—proud most of all of the promptness with which they were presented. It wasn't until the age of five, when I first visited our Hartford relatives, that I discovered what the rest of the world considered to be toast. Her cooking of chicken, steak, or roasts (almost anything, now that I think of it) involved that same adherence to the principle of preparation well in advance of consumption. She would begin the roasting or broiling of meat for dinner as soon as the breakfast dishes were put away. Throughout the day, the food was placed in the refrigerator for safekeeping, and then triumphantly reheated a couple of hours before we seated ourselves at table. When the meat course appeared, warmed anew, it was diminished in size, lacking in color, and devoid of aroma. The texture was that of dry clay. Unless one was ravenous, the food was swallowed with difficulty, although my father seemed to thrive on it, perhaps out of habit, and depended on its predictability.

During the evening meal, Jennie patrolled the table, checking on one's rate and volume of consumption. If most of the food was left uneaten on the plate, she would remedy the situation by approaching the offending plate with a salt shaker and say, "Have some salt"—at which point one would have some salt whether one wanted it or not. As soon as any edible on the plate disappeared, it would be instantly replaced by another portion. There was, it seemed, an infinite supply of the evening's fare in her kitchen; her meals were more than enough for twice the number of diners present. Food to her was meant to be eaten in copious amounts, not necessarily enjoyed for its taste. This conception of dining was especially apt for her children, whom she considered to be "skinny pickles." We

155

were thin kids (perhaps because of her cuisine), but her
nightly commands of "Eat! Eat!" didn't make us any chub-
bier. For a long time, the three of us referred to her simply
as "Eat."

Once in a while, one of our various maids would be
permitted to cook a meal. However, any maid's culinary
touch was dulled by Jennie's close supervision, which demanded the chilling-reheating procedure until all taste had
been banished. But I am being thankless—"a rotten kid,"
as my mother often put it. She cooked a few dishes well.
One, really. It was a Russian-Jewish treat called *goleptses*
—spicy chopped meat wrapped in slippery cabbage leaves
and served in a tart raisin gravy—which Jennie had learned
how to make from her mother, Pearl. (Pearl, by all accounts, was a superb cook, but her skill was inherited only
by one daughter, Dorothy.) The announcement of *goleptses* on the evening menu was cause for great rejoicing,
and this reaction so pleased Jennie that she scheduled the
dish at least once a week. Then she grew suspicious. Why
did we like *goleptses* so much? What was wrong with her
other dishes? We never told her.

The bulk of my envisioned "The Jennie Bernstein Cookbook" was to be anecdotes, not recipes: anecdotes about
Jennie and Sam in collision with their new world. For instance, Jennie had decided in the early nineteen-fifties that
while she was more knowledgeable about music through
her concertgoing, she should improve her understanding
of fine arts, too. She was intuitively appreciative of good
paintings and sculpture, as she certainly was of good
music, but she was at a loss in expressing her appreciation,
and so she enrolled in a course at Boston's Museum of Fine
Arts. Part of the curriculum was to gain awareness of technique by actually painting with oils. Jennie liked the painting best of all. Once, when she was asked how her lessons
at the museum were going, she replied, "It's wonderful!
I'm already in my Cuban phase." Later on, she began to

paint at home, setting up her easel and materials in a room in our Brookline house with a view due west to a wooded ridge. For weeks, we all watched a major interior-exterior painting take shape—what looked to our conventional eyes like the sun hovering over the ridge line as seen through the window, with part of the room in the foreground. But there was a puzzling white rectangular area around the bright-yellow ball of the sun, which I assumed meant something rather esoteric (maybe even "Cuban"). When she declared the painting finished, I complimented her on the interesting colors and composition, but I couldn't restrain myself from asking about the significance of the white rectangle around the sun. "The sun?" she said. "What sun? That's the brass knob on the closet door. It's a still-life." She could be just as dumbfounding in her appreciation of architecture. When Felicia was showing her the quaint gingerbread-house façades of Oak Bluffs, on Martha's Vineyard, Jennie studied the ornate fronts and said, "Typical Gay Thirties." Ever since, the Gay Thirties School of Art has been our family favorite.

As her exposure to the strange world of intellectuals and artists increased, Jennie, I suppose, came to believe that she should offer more profound opinions—more profound, say, than "I thought it was very nice, dear." In her mind, the road to profundity was paved with reckless generalizations (perhaps *because* of her exposure to intellectuals and artists), and soon the wild, all-inclusive statement became a Jennie trademark. Her broader declarations often concerned "you New Yorkers," as opposed to "us Bostonians." If a person who lived in New York said he thought that Stravinsky's "Le Sacre du Printemps" was a powerful work, Jennie would chime in with something like, "Oh, you New Yorkers love your Stravinsky. In Boston, we like our Tchaikovsky." Or, if it was snowing in Boston and fair in New York Jennie could be counted upon to say during a phone call when weather was discussed, "It's always snowing in Boston;" if the reverse was true, "It's always snowing in New York." Her finest, and most often recounted, generalization took place at a formal gathering that was delayed slightly by the tardy arrival of a gentleman who happened to be French-Canadian. When the man finally entered the room, he apologized for being late and explained that he had to entertain some guests who had dropped in on him unexpectedly. "Oh, you French-Canadians, you just love to entertain," Jennie said, not at all sarcastically. A moment of dreadful silence followed that enormous pronouncement, and Jennie sensed that she had made a gaffe. At last, she broke the tension by adding, "Just like the Israelis."

Her generalizations were sometimes combined with idioms of her own invention. She once told me that a particular bill had been "paid down."

"Don't you mean 'paid up'?" I said.

"No, 'paid down,' " she insisted. "That's the way we say it in Boston."

When I turned forty, she wrote me a touching, consoling letter, which ended, "Don't feel bad about being forty. Remember, you're still my sibling." And when she telephoned to invite me to the dedication of the gravestone for a deceased brother-in-law, Jennie said, "Your Aunt Dorothy is unveiling her husband next week." And after Lenny once spoke movingly about freedom during a Seder, Jennie's voice was heard exclaiming, "I second the emotion."

But her cultural allusions were the most noteworthy. On a valentine card to my son, Michael, she wrote: "Michael, how many ways I love you! Let's count the ways. Love, Grandma Browning." And there was the time she realized her wallet was missing from her purse after a concert at Lincoln Center. Shirley took charge of the search for the wallet, and, several anxious hours later, it was found, intact. Too exhausted by the effort of the search to coin an original phrase, Shirley simply sighed and said, "All's well that ends well," to which Jennie added, "Shakespeare couldn't have said it better."

Whenever Jennie employed a cliché, it seldom failed to surprise. She once wished me well on a forthcoming book and said she hoped that it would "sell like hot potatoes." On another such occasion, she said she hoped that the new book would "sell in the hundreds." (It did.) She once refused a slice of extremely rich cake by saying, "That cake, you couldn't sell it to me!" And of taking a plane from Boston to New York she said, quite seriously, "I'm not so crazy about flying anymore. Flying is for the birds." There was no question that her humorous lines were unintentional, because as those around her lost control and snickered she would merely stare in wonder at the reaction; then she would join in the laughter herself.

If Jennie's misuse of the cliché evoked hard-to-suppress general amusement, Sam's caused general hilarity. He was the all-time master of what I suppose could be called the mixed cliché, or the nearly accurate one. When he was ill, for example, he would complain about getting "sidekicks from the medicine." In 1966, he abruptly halted negotiations for the sale of his business, because at the last moment he "got cold shoulders." An unfamiliar person he didn't know "from a hole in the head." During summer thunderstorms, it was invariably "raining dogs outside." For someone who was departing on a long trip, Sam bought "a getaway present." He would fly from Boston to New York on "the shuffle." His most respected business associate was "a very clean and cut fellow," who spared no expense on Sam and Jennie whenever they met him in "Flarda," as Sam called it. "Oh, how he song and danced us in Miami," Sam once reported. Important people whom he encountered on trips were always "very famous but I wouldn't want to indulge their names." And as far back as I can recall my father guarded against the vagaries of fate by advising, "Keep your finger crossed."

Family Matters

I've long believed that the most iridescent gem of Samiana or Jenniana took place in Los Angeles, while Lenny was conducting on the West Coast in 1960. Jennie and Sam had never been to California, so Lenny invited them to meet him there. It was a special thrill for Jennie, who, as I've noted, had been infatuated with shopgirl movies and their stars ever since her girlhood. Indeed, she had named her daughter Shirley Anne, after, in a roundabout fashion, the child-star Anne Shirley. Tout Hollywood fêted Lenny and his parents during their stay, and Jennie was in a glassy-eyed daze as her favorite film personalities made much of her at glittering Beverly Hills parties. At one gala, Jennie spotted the actress Anita Louise across the room and tentatively approached her. "Oh, Anita Louise," Jennie said to her, "you've always been my favorite. You know, I named my daughter, Shirley, after you."

*L*ENNY'S SUDDEN FAME, OF course, also had its peculiar impact on Shirley and me. For one thing, it separated us even more from our parents, while it brought the three children closer together than ever. Shirley and I were exposed to people, places, and ideas whose existence we had only dimly acknowledged before November of 1943. Lenny liked to have us around him to share in it all—art, urbane conversation, celebrities, show business, travel—and Shirley, particularly, relished the opportunity. The pretty, bright girl who had been named after Anne Shirley (or Anita Louise, as the case may be) was ready for, and vulnerable to, those seductive orbits around Lenny. At the time of his début, Shirley had almost finished her formal education and was aching to be set loose in the world, but not the world that Jennie and Sam had planned for her—a return to Boston, a marriage

to a nice, steady chap (who might be eager for a partner-
ship in a going beauty-supplies concern), and a long life in
a happy home filled with nice, steady children. But that
was not to be.

Perhaps it was inevitable that Shirley's future would be
inextricably entangled with Lenny's. Since her childhood,
she had been under his spell—a kid sister who looked upon
him not only as a big brother but as a kind of father, too.
The attraction of her imaginative, charming, pedagogic,
talented older brother was overpowering. Part of the reason
for this closeness to Lenny was her place in the family
structure, an unfortunate legacy from the Old Country.
She was a girl child, the second born, of whom nothing
much was expected or demanded save the *nachas* that
comes from her being one day a good homemaker and a
bearer of children—after she was suitably educated, of
course. Not that she wasn't loved by Jennie and Sam. They
adored her, but not quite in the same way that they adored
Lenny. And when I was born—another son, the baby of
their middle years—Shirley's status slipped badly. She was
caught in a familial limbo: she was neither the oldest nor
the youngest, no longer the cutest or the cuddliest, and
certainly not the center of attention. She was the daughter
in the middle.

Shirley's early relationship with Jennie and Sam was erratic. While there was a firm mother-daughter bond—having little female chats, cooking, knitting, and shopping
together—Jennie's time was severely restricted when I
came along, and Shirley was often left to her own devices.
(One result of this isolation was a classic case of sibling
jealousy. Shirley got even with her innocent newborn
brother by experimentally depressing the fontanel on his
infant head, until his screams frightened her off. Later, she
convinced him that she was really his mother and that
Jennie was his grandmother. When he ran crying to Jennie
for what he hoped would be a strong denial of the treach-

erous calumny, Jennie would say, in an offhand way, "Of course not, dear. Don't listen to that pest Shirley." He half-believed Shirley's mean tale for one difficult year.)

The daughter's feelings about her father were problematical. "On the one hand," Shirley has told me, "I saw Daddy as a tyrant—not so much to me as to Mama. The tension in the house was palpable. He frightened me, because I never knew when he was going to whirl on Mama. The words between them were sometimes ugly, and the silences were just as ugly. I identified with Mama to the point where I vowed that I wouldn't live her life over again —and that's why I'm not married today, I guess. I remember swearing to myself, at eight or nine, that whatever happened to me, I won't have that life of a benumbed woman, the wife of a tyrant. I know that Daddy really loved me, but he showed affection with great difficulty. He rarely hugged me. Instead, he would ruffle my hair over my eyes —which had the effect on me that being rubbed the wrong way has on a cat. But, even with his bumbling manner, he could be very tender and sweet. If I was sick, he would fall all over himself with worry and trying to make me better. And he very tenderly taught me my bedtime prayers. When he was depressed and brooding, I was in tune with him, in a funny way—with his isolation, his feeling of being unloved. I felt so sorry for him. But he wouldn't let me get close enough to find out what the trouble was." This made for a somewhat difficult childhood. For a while, Shirley sleepwalked, appearing spookily at her mother's side in the middle of the night. She read voraciously to escape, both trashy books and classics, exhausting the fiction shelves of local libraries. She, like Sam, felt a bit left out of things.

Except with Lenny. Thanks to her older brother, she had become a charter citizen of Rybernia at age five, a trusted performer in his productions, somebody who could help him learn operas by singing the female roles, often until her vocal cords were inflamed. Lenny was the person to whom she went for help with her homework, for brotherly and paternal advice, for playing word games, for laughs. And when Lenny became famous there was no question in her mind that she would be part of his new life. At Mount Holyoke, Shirley had been in an accelerated-graduation program, a wartime expedient to make more room at the college for the training of WAVES. Until Lenny's début, she had intended to join the WAVES after her graduation. (The smart uniforms and the chance to be an active participant in the war effort were the major attractions.) However, she changed her mind about the WAVES once she had her diploma. To appease her parents, she said that she would live with them in the new Brookline house. It was a tiny deception. She moved in for a few weeks in the winter of 1944, but before long she persuaded Jennie and Sam that Lenny desperately needed a secretary and that she would be perfect for the job once she had polished up her typing. Despite parental misgivings, she moved to New York and shared Lenny's apartment.

As a secretary, Shirley was less than efficient, but as a companion and a sort of concert valet she was valuable. (Lenny soon acquired the efficient services of his former piano teacher Helen Coates for the burgeoning secretarial chores, and she has performed those tasks ever since.) Shirley delighted in the theatrical world and the swirl of celebrities around Lenny. I would receive newsy, envy-making letters from her with information such as this:

Lenny and Sylvia Lyons gave a great party the other night— all the usual people plus, mind you, Ethel Barrymore, Bernard Baruch, Joe DiMaggio, Charles Boyer, Ezio Pinza, Moss Hart, John Steinbeck, Garson Kanin, Al Hirschfield, Abe Burrows, Frank Loesser, John Ringling North—and people like that there; how about that?

It wasn't long before she entered show business herself, with Lenny's help. A gritty, bluesy song called "Big Stuff," which Lenny had written to set the scene for his first ballet, "Fancy Free," required a gritty, bluesy voice. Shirley's chronically inflamed vocal cords produced a quality just right for a recording of the song, a few bars of which sounded before the opening moment of the ballet. And when Lenny and choreographer Jerome Robbins expanded the three-sailors-on-shore-leave theme into the musical "On the Town" (with book and lyrics by Betty Comden and Adolph Green), Shirley was cast in the singing chorus. She stayed with the show until 1946, finally being promoted to a small speaking role. From then on, it was all show business, in one way or another. Her performing career faded —she was self-critical enough to realize that her talents were limited—but she entered the area of theatrical and television production with spirit and talent. Most recently, she has formed her own literary agency. But her involvement in Lenny's life has remained constant, even after his marriage to Felicia, in 1951. Why she would prefer that "crazy-artist" world in New York to stable Boston and marriage, home, and family was a puzzle to Jennie and Sam, but one they never quite gave up the hope of solving.

*A*S FOR THE KID BROTHER, the unexpected departure of Shirley for New York in 1944 left me feeling deserted: another member of my other family, my Rybernian family, had flown the coop, and I was suddenly an only child. I loved my parents, and they loved me—doted on me, in fact—but I still felt deserted. Lenny and Shirley were off in New York; I was stuck at home, just another grammar-school kid.

Actually, my sense of forlornness wasn't all that sudden. It had begun around 1940, when Lenny went to the Curtis

Institute and Shirley entered Mount Holyoke, but then they at least used to come home fairly regularly. Despite the large age differences, especially between Lenny and me, I had always been close to them. They enjoyed going beyond the usual big-brother and big-sister roles, sharing their private thoughts, jokes, and language with little Baudumü. Lenny never tired of instructing me in such intricate matters as the facts of life, music appreciation, political science, and just about anything he happened to learn at school. In a sense, I received a secondhand Harvard education, starting at the age of three. I doubt that his patient instruction made me any more intelligent than my coevals, but it did seem to stimulate my young imagination. With my miniature carpenter's set, I would retire to my room for hours on end to construct not just crude boxes but entire automobiles and airplanes, capable of being sat in. And I sang while I hammered and sawed— naughty ditties my sister taught me to shock Jennie and Sam, and my own lyrics to such numbers as Beethoven's "Pastoral" Symphony. (To the "Shepherd's Song" theme of the last movement, I would intone: "Sometimes it's raining before our work and play/ Sometimes it's raining— we're glad to say, 'Good morning.' . . .") To keep me company in my solitary pursuits, I had three very dear imaginary friends, named, for no special reason, Greena Gom, Bob Vrom, and Smooth. The four of us would have lengthy conversations about life in general and carpentry in particular. As I recall, Greena and Bob were nice, ordinary children, but Smooth was deceitful. (Lenny's first luxury car was an enormous forest-green 1947 Buick convertible, which was christened "Greena," in honor of my old friend.)

My frequent childhood illnesses and the accompanying confinements to bed also stimulated my inventiveness. It seemed that I was a victim of one continuous cold, despite "Dr. Finky"'s inoculations and my father's constant in-

junction "Button up your neck!" In midwinter, my unend-
ing cold would erupt into sieges of pneumonia, bronchitis,
and ear infections. Whenever I was in danger of wasting
away to nothing, Sam would pack Jennie and me off to
Florida, where, according to "Dr. Finky," all ailments
could be cured by "putting your nose in the sun." The
better part of two winters spent in a dreary Miami Beach
hotel helped somewhat. To amuse myself in Miami among
all those infirm, aging adults, I would write stories in the
school notebooks that I was given by my teachers in order
to practice the multiplication tables I was not learning back
home. One story, in its entirety, reads:

THE MOTHER GOOSE MURDER
Lennord Burton was sitting in his room in his stoudio. He was
so busy dreaming he did not notice the window open. All of the
sudden a package dropped on the floor. It startled Lennord he
jumped up in surprise. He saw the man jump away but did not
go after him because the other man had a good start. He looked
on the floor and he saw a jack in the box on the floor. He picked
it up. He pushed the Button and Pop a little head poped out. He
pushed the head back into the box again. There was an boom. A
cop on the corner came up and came in what was left of the
room and there on the floor was Jim. Dead.

However much my creativity flowered during those two
winters in the semitropics, my schooling suffered. But
when I returned to the John Ward School, in Newton—
tanned, a little more flesh on my bones, still sniffling—I
managed to catch up with the rest of my class and be promoted. One of my teachers, Rachel Stein, described the
situation in a letter to my parents:

May 24, 1940
DEAR MR. & MRS. BERNSTEIN,
Since Grade III marks the end of a period in your child's
growth, and Grade IV begins a new educational cycle, we are

The Kids

sending you information concerning his achievement up to this time. We are attempting to give you a clear picture of your child's development. . . .

Burtie loves to read, and he does this very well. He equally enjoys our discussion periods and is always anxious to make his contribution. He holds the interest of the group, and finds it easy to tell what he has read in his own words.

Arithmetic and spelling seem to require more effort, but he is willing to work, and so I can see no reason that he should encounter any great difficulties.

It has always been a pleasure to have Burtie so interested in his work. Sometimes, however, his enthusiasm becomes so intense that he finds himself working under great pressure and strain. A little guidance, at this point, is very valuable to him, and he soon gets control of himself.

Because of this high sense of enthusiasm, Burtie has not always found it easy to do his work carefully and accurately. Papers have come in very untidy and hastily done. It has been good, however, to see a steady improvement along this line, and now, more regularly, his work assumes a different tone quality.

Burtie likes to play—in boyish fashion—and often does not make the most of his time.

Burtie is popular with the group, and all were eager to have him return from his trip to Florida. He is a good sport—he loves to win, and yet he can lose with a smile.

I have enjoyed working with Burtie.

Sincerely yours,
RACHEL STEIN

As Miss Stein indicated in her progress report, I was a fairly normal American boy, despite my secret citizenship in Rybernia and long periods of lonely convalescence. I had close boyfriends, a few comely girlfriends, a reputation for excellence in running sports, and three consecutive mongrel dogs, all answering to "Mippy" (after Ambrose Mippy, the inventor of the shoehorn in a funny Revuers' sketch; it was a knotty task to explain the dogs' name to those who were not acquainted with the work of Betty Comden and Adolph Green, and those unfortunates were legion then). In truth, the dogs were my mother's. She loved them most and cared for them best, and the dogs knew it. They rarely let her out of their sight, and they growled at anyone who approached her stealthily, even me. But, alas, all the dogs ended badly—run over, stolen, lost. When the third Mippy escaped from a boarding kennel, where we had put him before one of our trips to New York, and never reappeared, Jennie tearfully said to me, "I have no luck with your dogs." Sam, too, loved the Mippys, even to the extreme of confusing them with his children. In distracted moments, he would call to me, running the gamut of his offspring's names: "Lenny . . . Shirley . . . Mippy . . . *Burtie!*"

Those wholesome aspects of a more or less normal boyhood were compromised in 1941 when Sam sold the Newton house and we moved permanently to our newly enlarged house in Sharon. Sharon in the summer was a happy, warm place, but I soon learned that a not-so-subtle change came over the town in the winter months. Many of the locals, who tolerated and profited from the Jewish summer residents of the Grove, were in reality unabashed anti-Semites—because, I suppose, of that seasonal economic dependency and a lingering resentment of the strange-talking, well-heeled interlopers from the city, descendants, they were told, of the murderers of Christ. This hostility was decorously hidden by the adults in their dealings with my parents, but their children—especially the preadolescents of my age group—were far less restrained. I discovered this on my first day at school. A burly lout named Arthur decided that "the new Jew kid" would require his permission to board the yellow school bus. I looked to the driver for help, but he stared out his windshield, muttering, "Come on, you people, let's go." I elbowed my way past

Arthur and caught his lunch box on my head for my daring. As I sat hunched and alone on a bus seat meant for two passengers, Arthur and some of his friends threw banana peels, erasers, and spitballs at me. It was the worst day of my young life. I didn't tell my parents about it.

Taking the yellow bus to and from school each weekday became so painful, physically and emotionally, that I walked or rode my Schwinn bicycle the three miles whenever the weather permitted. Inside the school, I wasn't bothered much—just generally ignored. I retreated inward, no longer displaying that "high sense of enthusiasm" that Miss Stein had detected in the Newton classroom. One Sharon teacher was alarmed enough by my sullen silence to call in Jennie for a conference; they decided that it was just a phase I was going through, intensified by the change of school. But on Monday morning, December 8, 1941, the day after Pearl Harbor was attacked, the school itself became as dangerous for me as the bus. We fifth graders were standing in the cold, wet recess yard, waiting to enter the dismal school building. My nemesis, Arthur, worked his way into line behind me and proclaimed loudly, "My father says it was the Jap-Jews that bombed us, and this guy is one of them." He shoved me hard and chanted "Jap-Jew, Jap-Jew," and the chant was taken up by several other kids. I doubt that any American nine-year-old boy was more concerned about the war than I was. I had carefully followed the bloody progress of the Nazis on my father's pin-stuck battle map, I had read the war news every day in the Boston *Herald*, and I had stayed up late with my parents the night before to hear the horrendous reports on the radio about the sneak Japanese attack on Hawaii. Nobody was going to call me a "Jap-Jew," whatever the hell that was. I lunged for Arthur and hit him twice in the face before he and a couple of other boys knocked me down onto the asphalt pavement and pummelled me. When a teacher finally stopped the beating, my face was covered with blood and tears. It was my uncontrollable, convulsive sobbing that worried and humiliated me most. It continued throughout the morning—in the nurse's office (where I was washed and painted with iodine), in the principal's office (where I was blamed for the sneak attack on Arthur), and, later, in my mother's car (where I found myself being driven home, after she was called to the school by the principal). When I told her my side of the story, she comforted me and said, "I knew we shouldn't have moved from Newton." Sam said the same thing when he came home that night, but the way he put it was "Why did you let me sell the Newton house, Jennie?" His guilt threw him into a depression that lasted for days. I frequently overheard them talking about sending me to a boarding school.

There were a few more fights with Arthur and some others, but they were less virulent than the Pearl Harbor incident. At last, I was just generally ignored again, except by two friends I had won—Eddie Parker and Marjorie Jones. Eddie Parker was a sickly kid from a pious Catholic family. We became good friends because he stepped in to help me in one of my fights; he said that his mother had told him it would be the right thing to do. Eddie, his mother, his whole family were like that. When he was absent from school, I would take his homework over to his house and study with him. Sometimes he'd be absent for weeks on end, and I'd be a semipermanent fixture at his place, sharing the Parkers' meals and doing some of Eddie's chores. Marjorie Jones, who sat next to me in homeroom, was pert and popular. She liked to pass notes during class, and she thought that my scribbles were amusing. We were caught once and had to stay after school together, washing blackboards. From then on, I had a large crush on her, although our relationship seldom went beyond the note-passing stage. At school assemblies, when we were supposed to raise our voices in Protestant hymns (as well as "Praise the

The Kids

Lord and Pass the Ammunition!" and "America, the Beautiful"), I could never quite bring myself to sing out the ringing last line of the doxology—"Praise Father, Son, and Holy Ghost." Instead, I used to mumble, "Praise Father, Son, and Marjorie Jones."

Besides my two friends, I took comfort in ice hockey and, oddly enough, the war during those Sharon winters. Once I had learned how to play hockey, I was pretty much accepted as a regular guy—even, grudgingly, by Arthur, who released his remaining hostility on the ice with bruising but clean body checks. We Sharon boys were so enamored of hockey that we shovelled the snow off the lake ice before we shovelled out our driveways—a practice that did not please our parents. The thrill of scoring a goal, of colliding with another kid out of sport, not meanness, helped me gain confidence with my fellows and in school.

As for the war, it captured most of my waking thoughts and whatever imagination I had left. I spent Saturday mornings collecting scrap metal, flattened tin cans, old tires, and newspapers for the war effort, and later I earned the position of junior airplane spotter for the Massachusetts State Guard—a collection of overage men who packed unloaded shotguns and wore First World War uniforms on weekend maneuvers. To facilitate my spotter duty, I was given an official chart showing the silhouettes and characteristics of all the American, British, German, Japanese, and Italian planes, and I committed these to memory. We never identified anything in the Sharon skies other than American aircraft, but, as we used to say so solemnly out in the woods on fair weekend afternoons, you never know when some suicidal Nazi bastard might fly his Messerschmitt-109 over Sharon, Mass., do you? (Rumors of secret Nazi airfields in the Canadian wilderness were rife.) It was my unashamed dream to be an American fighter pilot, the sole master of a screaming P-47, its fifty-calibre machine guns spitting fiery lead at the accursed enemy. And un-

171

ashamed, too, was my fervent hope that the war would last
long enough for me to be of eligible age to join the Army
Air Forces. Until that glorious day, I would have to content
myself with constructing models of fighters and drawing
flaming dogfights (the Messerschmitt-109's and Zeros flaming most) in my schoolbooks. I had mixed feelings on V-J
Day, when I was just a hopelessly underage thirteen.

An inevitable result of my three full-time years in Sharon
was my discomfort at being Jewish. It surfaced in two ways:
my stubborn reluctance to learn Hebrew in preparation for
my forthcoming bar mitzvah, and embarrassment over my
father's accent and his annoying habit of seeing everything
through a Jewish lens. The effect of my behavior on Sam
was devastating; it was unthinkable that his son wouldn't
be an exemplary Jewish lad. Even rebellious Lenny had
been faultless in that department. Once, when I told my
father that, on intellectual grounds, it would be hypocriti-
cal of me, a nonbeliever, to go with him to *shul* on Yom
Kippur, he turned crimson and threatened me with all
kinds of punishments. Just before I relented, he shouted,
"Even the goyim go to *shul* on Yom Kippur!" Who could
refuse him after that? But my private anti-Semitism pre-
vailed, even unto my sham bar mitzvah in the marble halls
of Temple Mishkan Tefila. I did learn by rote the ritual
prayers and the required Scriptural passages, and I carried
off the ceremony with dignity and panache—a good bluff
job. My parents' friends were duly impressed; another
Bernstein son had shown himself to be a fine Hebrew
scholar, a credit to his people. Little did they know. After
the bar mitzvah, my discomfort gradually disappeared, but
my spiritual feeling for the Jewish religion, any religion,
never seems to have been there in the first place.

Adolescence struck about the time we moved to Brookline, just after Lenny's sensational début. Mine was probably no worse than any other twelve-year-old boy's.
Scholastic and social enthusiasms returned with their old

The Kids

intensity, and because my brother was famous I had a certain cachet among my contemporaries and teachers. (When "On the Town" tried out in Boston, in late 1944, I was elevated to a kind of celebrity myself.) But the difference between most adolescents and me was that I had *two* families to rebel against—especially those two fathers, Sam and Lenny. In Sam's case, I denied the causes closest to his heart—his religion and his business. When he maneuvered me into attending services at Mishkan Tefila, I would slip away to the Franklin Park Zoo, across the street, during the rabbi's sermons. I was a "rotten kid," all right, but I rationalized my rottenness by claiming moral and intellectual integrity. I knew I was hurting Sam, but I couldn't seem to help myself. When he tried to interest me in the beauty-supplies business, I wounded him just as deeply. He wanted me to learn the business from the bottom up, working on Saturdays and during school vacations as a delivery boy and a packer in the shipping room, but after a while I so upset the other employees with my snide remarks about commerce that even Sam thought it best for me to spend my free time in some other enterprise, like shovelling snow or raking leaves. As far as his business was concerned, all three of his children were ungrateful wretches.

My rebellion against Lenny took a similar tack, in that I tended to sneer at his world. Anything connected with long-hair music and art was beneath my notice—sissy stuff. Part of this attitude wasn't necessarily my fault. In greenrooms after Lenny's concerts, well-meaning but thoughtless people would ask me, "Are you going to be a famous conductor, too?" At first, I answered politely (forcing a smile and examining my shoes: "No, I don't think so"), but as that dreaded question became more frequent and predictable my responses grew ruder (brightly: "No, I'm going to be an osteopath"). Actually, more than ever I wanted to be a P-47 pilot. But until that time I had to be satisfied with any kind of speed—running the hundred-yard dash ever faster, tearing down hills on my Schwinn bike and applying the brakes only at the last second, skating and skiing heedlessly, racing my motorboat on Massapoag Lake, purloining the family Oldsmobile and seeing what it could do on desolate country roads. Speed, athletic or mechanical, seemed to me as contrary to artistic endeavor as anything could possibly be. It was virile, exciting, perilous, and, best of all, nobody in my family approved of it.

No matter how fast I sped, it was nothing compared with what I imagined flying would be. I had never been up in an airplane, but from building my models and diligently reading Antoine de Saint-Exupéry and technical books I thought I knew as much about aviation as most licensed pilots did. I arrogantly assumed that I could simply get into a Piper J-3 Cub and take off, without a minute of formal instruction. Strangely, it was Lenny, the consummate artist, who introduced me to my first experience of flight. In the early summer of 1946, he visited Sharon, the scene of his youthful triumphs, before he went off to Tanglewood, where he was teaching and conducting. He was full of stories about his more recent triumphs, all of which I greeted with calculated indifference, but one of his tales brought me up sharp. Some new acquaintance had taken Lenny for a spin in a small plane and had let him handle the controls. He described the thrill of flying in such a poetic way that I lost all pretense of adolescent coolness. I was jealous. That afternoon, without telling anybody, we drove to nearby Norwood Airport, a former military-training base that had been converted into a private field and flying school after the war. (I had previously spent many afternoons standing by the fence of that airport watching the little yellow Piper Cubs land and take off.) Lenny said that he wanted to take a lesson and that he'd treat me to one, also. He went up first, in a J-3 Cub, with an instructor. An hour later, they landed, and Lenny was ecstatic. "Wait until you try it," he said. "You'll never be the same again." He was absolutely right. After that first lesson, I vowed that I would be a pilot, no matter what.

However, my second lesson didn't take place for more than a year later—a year spent trying to convince my parents that flying was as harmless as riding a bike. They weren't convinced, and since lessons cost eight dollars an hour—money, Sam made quite clear, he would not provide—they reasoned that my infatuation was not practicable, anyway. But I found odd jobs, saved my allowance and school-lunch money, and finally accumulated enough cash to pay for the necessary instruction leading up to my first solo. Sam was struck by my initiative, as he had been by Lenny's financing his piano lessons, and he gave me permission to fly. Jennie, however, was terrified. I told her that she should see for herself how safe it was. So persuasive was my argument (I had Lenny's old wheedling technique down pat) that she drove me to the Norwood Airport for my second lesson, and sat in the car with her eyes shut, a prayer on her lips, while I took off in a flimsy, fabric-covered Cub. When I returned to the car, intoxicated by the magic of controlled flight, she said, "O.K., fly—but don't ever ask me to come here again." Flying, my parents figured, was something I'd get out of my system—like Lenny and his music—if I didn't kill myself first. They were right, but it took many years and a lot of magical flights. I still get a funny feeling when I'm near a small plane. Indeed, in the past year I've taken up private flying again.

During that summer of 1946, Lenny was responsible for another crucial moment in my life, one that had the effect of extinguishing my rebellion—against him, at any rate. He invited me to come to Tanglewood and stay as long as I liked at his rented cottage, on the shore of the Stockbridge Bowl. It was the first full-blown season of the Berkshire Music Center after the war, and the central event was the American première of Benjamin Britten's opera "Peter Grimes," which had been commissioned by Koussevitzky (and was called by its sponsor "Peter *und* Grimes"). Koussevitzky had designated Lenny to be the conductor of the opera, a complex work that tested the talents of the Opera Department.

When I arrived at Lenny's cottage (with the intention of staying for just a few days), I walked into a winning bedlam, the likes of which I had never seen before. Besides Lenny, Helen Coates, and a maid as the permanent inhabitants, there was a procession of transients: Shirley; Adolph Green and his fiancée, Allyn Ann McClerie; Betty Comden and her husband, Steve Kyle; Judy Holliday; Jerome Robbins; the pianist William Kapell; the composer David Diamond; various other musicians; and Lenny's girlfriend, a petite Chilean actress named Felicia Montealegre. Despite my noble intentions and philistine pose, I was captivated by the delightful chaos and all those "crazy artist nuts," as Sam called them. I stayed on and on that summer, working as a lighting technician in the "Peter Grimes" production. At fourteen, I was certainly the youngest student at Tanglewood and everybody's pet. And I had discovered a new element, almost as much fun as speed and flying. I learned about opera and stagecraft and poetry and literature and crazy artists and the way special minds work. I became hooked on a world that I presumably loathed.

Of all the people crammed into Lenny's lakeshore cottage that summer, Felicia was the one who beguiled me most. I had first met her the previous spring, when she had come to Boston with Lenny for one of his concerts there, and we had become good friends. What instantly attracted me to her then—beyond her delicate beauty, her humor and spirit, and her lilting, unidentifiable accent, which, with her little black beret, evinced an intriguing foreignness —was her *not* asking me in the Symphony Hall greenroom whether I was going to be a famous conductor, too. Of such small civilities are great relationships born. Lenny had brought her to Boston primarily to meet Jennie and Sam.

Felicia and he were something of an item in New York. They had been introduced to each other by the Chilean pianist Claudio Arrau, who was Felicia's mentor when she contemplated becoming a concert pianist after her arrival in America. (She soon realized that her higher talent was acting, and within a few years she was a leading lady of television drama.) Although the question of marriage had not yet arisen, Lenny thought that Jennie and Sam should meet her, just in case it did some day. From the parents' point of view, there would be problems with Felicia. True, she was half Jewish—her father was Roy Cohn, a California engineer who had settled in Chile—but her mother, the former Clemencia Montealegre, was a Latin-American aristocrat who had insisted on a strict Catholic upbringing for her three daughters. Consequently, Felicia had been educated by nuns in Santiago. Although the rebel of her convent school, she was hectored by conflicting religious forces throughout her life. Supreme *nachas* for Jennie and Sam meant a good Jewish marriage for Lenny as much as for Shirley, but Felicia was not the wife they had in mind for their famous son. From the start, a wariness enveloped them and Felicia. It dissipated somewhat when her engagement to Lenny was announced, at the end of 1946, but my parents and Felicia never really knew what to make of one another.

That was not the case with Felicia and me. During the "Peter Grimes" summer, it was as if I had been presented with a second older sister—one who even understood Rybernian, after a fashion. My counter-family had been increased by one. But toward the end of the following summer at Tanglewood (I worked as a lighting technician in the Opera Department for three successive seasons) Lenny and Felicia decided that neither of them was ready for marriage, and the engagement was broken off. Next to the principals, I was the most upset.

Another result of those Tanglewood summers was my

improved status with my brother and sister. As I stumbled into young manhood, the physical differences in our respective ages disappeared until we were practically contemporaries—in spirit, anyway. No longer was I so much the kid brother (or the baby in the Rybernian family); I came to be accepted as an equal, whose thoughts and sensibilities were not necessarily met with indulgent smiles. I was encouraged to go on trips with them—at first, some of Lenny's shorter conducting tours and occasional vacation jaunts. (On one of the latter, a search for good skiing conditions in southern New England, Lenny and I were lost on a back road in Cornwall, Connecticut, and, seeking directions, we blundered into the home of James Thurber, a literary hero to both of us. Almost thirty years after that fortuitous meeting with Thurber, I wrote his biography.) I probably learned more on those trips than I was absorbing in the classrooms of Brookline High School.

After the 1948 Tanglewood season—when I was sixteen, a licensed driver and a licensed pilot—Lenny broached the idea of our navigating Greena, his sleek Buick convertible, to some isolated spot out West, where he could work without interruption on his second symphony, based on W. H. Auden's long poem "The Age of Anxiety." The British poet Stephen Spender happened to be visiting Tanglewood at that time, and he suggested that we accompany him to D. H. Lawrence's ranch, near Taos, New Mexico, which the novelist's widow had made available to various artists who craved seclusion. Spender was going out there to work on a new literary project, and he told us that there would be plenty of room for Lenny and me. This unlikely trio took to the road in blistering mid-August—Lenny and I sharing the driving, Spender sitting poetically taut in the back seat, like a reincarnation of Shelley, as we plunged westward. None of us was aware at the outset that the four new tires Lenny had bought for Greena were defective. Just outside Oneonta, New York, the first tire blew to smithereens as we careered down a hot highway. Several heart-stopping seconds later, we skidded to a dusty halt in a ditch, just short of a large, implacable elm tree. "Have we had a tyre burst?" Spender asked as Lenny and I, limbs aquiver, staggered out of the car to inspect the damage. (His pronunciation of the word demands the British spelling "tyre.") The question didn't deserve an answer. Spender watched us remove the pitiful shreds of rubber and the mangled wheel until he wearied of observing such witless, sweaty work. By the time we were tightening the bolts on the spare, he had discovered a shaded rill and, thumbing through a thin volume of verses, he was lost in thought and nature. In three more locations—Nashville, Tennessee; Amarillo, Texas; and Tucumcari, New Mexico—the remaining defective tires burst, with more or less the same resulting brushes with disaster. Each time, Spender mysteriously found a rill, or at least an irrigation ditch, beside which he mused or read poetry while we quivered, swore, and sweated. In Amarillo, when my patience with Spender's aloofness had worn thin, he explained why such events hardly disturbed him: he had been a fireman in London during the Blitz.

But mostly the motor trip to Taos and our week's stay at the Lawrence ranch were filled with good, witty conversation. Again, I learned a great deal, in spite of myself. Lenny used the Taos expedition as the setting for a chapter of his book "The Joy of Music." The chapter was called "Bull Session in the Rockies," being an aesthetic dialogue featuring L.B., L.P. (Lyric Poet), and Y.B. (Younger Brother). Here follows a typical passage:

L.P.: I'm afraid you're begging the question. Nobody has proposed that Beethoven leads all the rest solely because of his rhythm, or his melody, or his harmony. It's the combination—

L.B.: The combination of undistinguished elements? That hardly adds up to the gold-plated bust we worship in the conservatory concert hall! And the counterpoint—

Family Matters

Y.B.: Gum, anyone?

L.B.:—is generally of the schoolboy variety. He spent his whole life trying to write a really good fugue. And the orchestration is at times downright bad, especially in the later period when he was deaf. Unimportant trumpet parts sticking out of the orchestra like sore thumbs, horns bumbling along on endlessly repeated notes, drowned-out woodwinds, murderously cruel writing for the human voice. And there you have it.

L.P. *(in despair):* Y.B., I wish I didn't have to constantly keep reminding you about driving sanely!

Y.B.: You have just split an infinitive. *(But he slows down.)*

At the Lawrence ranch, high on a Rocky mountain, each of us fell into a daily routine: L.B. composing at a balky piano in the living room, L.P. taking long walks and then setting down his peripatetically inspired poetry, Y.B. making friends with a neighboring Indian tribe and attempting to corral some half-wild ponies. At six o'clock every evening, we broke off whatever we were doing and bathed in an icy stream. Then, as the sun disappeared behind a russet ridge, Spender would sing, in a tentative, nasal way:

> *Now the day is over,*
> *Night is drawing nigh;*
> *Shadows of the evening*
> *Steal across the sky.*

And with that soaring adieu, the day would be over, save for dinner and some intellectual talk, punctuated by yawns. It was marvellous fun—the conversations, the Indians, the ponies, the pack rats, which stole your toothbrush and left a twig in its place, the erotic paintings by Lawrence on the walls, and even Lawrence's ashes and memorabilia in a musty outbuilding. But a week was all Lenny could take of the extreme isolation and the deficient piano. He and I sadly left Spender to the Lawrence ashes and the pack rats, and headed north to Sheridan, Wyoming, where we had been invited by a Tanglewood student to spend some time on his family's cattle ranch. We plunged into the strenuous Wyoming life, working, in effect, as hired ranch hands from dawn to dusk and then drinking beer in town at night with the local cowboys. It was a whole new adventure for both of us—a neat counterpoint to Spender, certainly—but soon it was back to the East for my last year of high school and Lenny's sixth year of growing fame. I considered myself to be a very lucky fellow.

After high school, there was Dartmouth, and in the summer of 1950, between my freshman and sophomore years, Lenny asked Shirley and me to keep him company on an extensive post-Tanglewood conducting tour of Europe. Shirley was between jobs and available, and I aborted a trans-America hitchhiking trip with a friend. From the moment we fastened our seat belts on the airliner to Paris, the three of us regressed to our old, puerile Rybernian form. The private jokes and allusions, the uncontrollable giggles and mad laughter, the infantile sense of sheer pleasure in one another's existence poured out nonstop, no matter how many eyebrows were raised in bemusement. It was difficult for the Europeans we encountered to fathom a brash, young American maestro who didn't use a baton and moved athletically on the podium; it was impossible for them to comprehend one who blended in quite happily with his dribbling siblings. Were we being vulgar Americans, loud Jews? We didn't care. Throughout the tour, it was as if there were only three people on earth and we were the fortunate trio.

The self-perpetuating fun carried us mindlessly through France, England, Scotland, Holland, West Germany, and Ireland. In Paris, where we stayed longest, Lenny was the *"chef d'orchestre distingué"* to everyone, and it was endlessly amusing to Shirley and me that the *"chef"*—our very own Lennuhtt—would mumble asides in Rybernian even as he was being lionized by some terribly grand *comtesse*. We could hardly wait to leave elegant receptions and special excursions to cultural landmarks so we could rush back to our hotel for some unmuffled jokes and, of all things, a long game of canasta. Canasta—loud, riotous, hysterical canasta—was the obsession of the tour. We played it not only in hotel rooms but in any enclosed space, secluded or otherwise: planes, trains, greenrooms at intermission, waiting rooms, lobbies, and, on one memorable occasion, a taxi speeding us across Ireland—the melds and packs balanced on laps and tucked into upholstery crevices, behind the rate card and the lap-robe holder, while the driver snatched astonished glances at us in his rearview mirror. Perhaps the zenith of our exclusive insanity (and rudeness) was our stay as guests in a Donegal castle. There, among British nobility, artists, and a deferential staff of deerstalkers, gillies, maids, chars, and an aged butler named Whiteside, we carried on as though we were in our own Sharon living room. Whiteside, we decided at first sight, was the original butler who did it, and he was promptly renamed Nightshade by us. He was a nice man, actually, and he kept us fortified with tea and scones during our enervating canasta tournaments.

Ireland was the last stop for me. Lenny and Shirley were going on to Italy and Israel, and I desperately wanted to stay with them, but I was late for my sophomore year at college as it was. When they saw me off on the plane at Shannon, it was a grievous parting. While we hadn't advanced the cause of American civilization much, we did have a spectacularly good time, a kind of last fling with our Rybernian childhood, our arrested development. We knew that sooner or later we three—especially *chef d'orchestre distingué*, thirty-two-year-old Lenny—would have to grow up, and that things would never be quite the same again.

The Kids

A LARGE PART OF GROWING up involved marriage and children. To those ends, Lenny had started seeing Felicia again in 1951. It was finally apparent to both of them that if they were ever going to marry, it would be to each other. In July of that year, at Tanglewood, their engagement was announced, for the second time in five years. In September, they were wed at Temple Mishkan Tefila, with two rabbis officiating. The ceremony and the ensuing reception, at our Brookline house, were at once tense and jubilant. Before the ceremony, Felicia had formally converted to Judaism—an action that left her mother, Clemencia, in a state of mild catatonia. Both Lenny and Felicia were approaching the frontier of that state themselves, as their mixed pasts appeared in a startling potpourri: various Chileans; Abe and Annie Miller; show-business friends; Sam's business associates and Sharon cronies; the Resnicks; and stunned Grandmother Dinah, on leave from the Hebrew Home for Aged. (For Dinah, the event was further proof of how utterly insane America was.) Sam and Jennie had swallowed hard, finally accepting Felicia and her background. Domestic *nachas* was the overriding factor; Lenny had a wife, and soon—please God—there would be grandchildren. They were thankful and sentimental.

Before long, there were grandchildren—in 1952, a girl, Jamie; in 1955, a boy, Alexander Serge (after, conversely, Serge Alexandrovich Koussevitzky); and, in 1962, another girl, Nina. Sam and Jennie took great pleasure in these more conventional rewards of family; they were fond of saying that Lenny's success meant little compared to a smile from firstborn Jamie, and it was probably true. The question of Shirley's singleness provoked frowns, but when

I married, in 1960, and gave them two more grandchildren, Karen and Michael, their appetite for *nachas* was almost sated. Almost.

Just as Sam and Jennie never totally gave up the hope that Shirley would "settle down with a nice fellow," they continued to hope that I would take over the family business, despite my firmly stated intentions to the contrary. At Dartmouth, I had decided that I would probably be a writer, not a pilot. At the Columbia University Graduate School of Journalism, I became sure of it. To hasten the day, I chose to be drafted for a two-year hitch in the Army rather than enlist for four years in the Air Force, though this would have fulfilled my old fighter-pilot dream. With the publication of my first book, Sam understood at last that there would be no inheritance of his business. What was by then an old Boston commercial establishment—a hard-won extension of himself; his fourth child, as it were —had become almost an orphan. Someday it would have to be adopted by a stranger. That realization was a body blow for him. The beauty trade had provided his three kids with a substantial life, but all three had turned their backs on it. Rotten kids.

*A*s THE COLD WAR GREW frigid in the nineteen-fifties, the letters from our Russian relatives arrived less frequently and then stopped altogether. Uncle Shlomo/Semyon had ceased writing directly to Sam much earlier, cautiously sending his stilted salutations via letters from cousin Mikhoel. (Similarly, Sam had sent *his* stilted salutations to his brother in letters to Mikhoel.) But with the rise of Nikita Khrushchev and the policy of peaceful coexistence, in the late fifties, the resulting thaw in American-Soviet relations was enough to allow for cultural exchanges and the opening of the American Exposition in Moscow. As part of President Eisenhower's Special International Program for Cultural Presentations, the New York Philharmonic was booked in the summer and early fall of 1959 for a sweeping tour of the Middle East and Europe, including nations behind the Iron Curtain. Lenny, who had been appointed music director of the Philharmonic in the fall of 1958, was looking forward particularly to his concerts in Russia. To set foot in the land of his forebears as the esteemed American leader of a distinguished American orchestra was the stuff of historical fiction. If he took Sam along with him to Russia and brought him together again with the only two close relatives who had survived the war—Shlomo (the brother whom Sam hadn't seen in more than fifty years) and Mikhoel (the nephew whom he had never seen)—that would really wrap up the saga: two brothers, choosing to follow the major divergent courses of the twentieth century, rising to the top, and then meeting again in their advanced years through the intercession of a son and nephew, a world-renowned musician. The symbolism of such a Pasternak-like plot, in a time of brightening hope for peace and understanding between two differing cultures, was irresistible.

Once Lenny had conceived this compelling notion, he cranked up the machinery for bringing it about. First, Sam had to be convinced that a trip to Russia would be the fulfilling adventure of his lifetime. (Jennie wanted no part of the adventure; she disliked long trips and had no desire to see Russia again.) When Lenny offered the invitation, Sam, buffeted by wildly conflicting emotions, asked to think about it for a while. For days, he paced the Brookline living room and thought. Did he want to return for a visit to the land he had fled? Yes and no. Could he stand the pain of confronting the demolished culture of his youth? Maybe yes, maybe no. Would the shock of seeing his brother again be too great? Perhaps. Several vacillating phone calls later, Sam finally announced, weakly, that he would go. Through pressure exerted by the State Department (which, in effect, was sponsoring the Philharmonic's tour), Sam received a Soviet tourist visa—not an easy document to obtain for a Russian native who had stolen across the border in 1908. Sam would fly from Boston to Paris on August 19th and then take a connecting flight to Moscow.

Just as complex were the arrangements at the other end. Soviet citizens needed specific permission to travel within their own country. In 1959, Shlomo was living the life of a retired mining engineer in Novosibirsk, in south-central Siberia, and Mikhoel worked and lived in Dnepropetrovsk, the Ukraine. Word simply couldn't be sent that their American relatives would be in Moscow, and would they kindly meet them at the Hotel Ukraina. Governmental consent and properly certified internal passports were required. But again the State Department successfully applied the right pressure in the right places. Lenny was assured that Shlomo Bernstein and Mikhoel Zvainboim would be allowed to come to Moscow. Then, at the beginning of August, just before Lenny was to leave for Greece to open his tour, he received another call from Sam. "I can't go," Sam said. "It's too much for me." Lenny understood. It probably was too much, emotionally. Sam, as he himself might have said, "got cold shoulders."

The Philharmonic tour was triumphant from the start, accomplishing its cultural and diplomatic goals. Lenny and Felicia sent me letters and postcards from the early stops in Greece, Turkey, Austria, and Poland, describing how thunderous the audiences were in their ovations, how the demands for encores were trying everyone. But all that éclat faded in comparison with the orchestra's reception in Russia. It was as if the entire nation had been waiting for the Americans' arrival. And somewhere among the distinguished well-wishers greeting Lenny were two men who identified themselves as Uncle Shlomo and Cousin Mikhoel.

They appeared at the Hotel Ukraina wearing ill-fitting Russian suits and nervous grins. "What I remember most about Shlomo was his mouthful of stainless-steel teeth," Lenny has said. "What a shock! He was big and muscular, a completely different type from Sam. Very sympathetic—smiling, outgoing. But those teeth! He had the look of a hardy Russian peasant, sort of like Khrushchev himself. I was thrilled to know there was such diversity in the family—as if I had come upon the legendary Bezalel, our giant blacksmith great-grandfather. Shlomo was unlike anybody else in the family I had ever met. We embraced, and I tried to talk with him in the little Russian I had picked up, but it was impossible. Finally, an interpreter appeared. Even so, Shlomo had very little to say. I asked him about his family, what he was doing, why he hadn't chosen to go to America, as Sam had. He answered that he was retired and living comfortably in Novosibirsk with his wife. He had only good things to say about his life in Russia—everything was hunky-dory. He seemed sincerely to like it where he was. As for the old *shtetl* where he and Sam grew up, he, too, had wanted to escape from it, but not to America. It was the new Russia that had attracted him. He wasn't the studious type, he told me—especially where Judaism was concerned. In fact, there was no sense of Jewishness about him at all. Just the opposite of Mikhoel, who was slight and resembled the Malamud side of the family. Mikhoel could speak Yiddish, and he had complaints. He was emotional. Life was difficult for him in Dnepropetrovsk. He couldn't be Jewish and worship there. I think that deep down he wanted to go to Israel. I was touched by him, but I felt no great connection with Shlomo, who had nothing substantial to tell me. Well, we did talk about Aunt Clara, his dead parents, America—but always on a superificial level. Noth-

ing important, like Clara's marriages and so forth. He
didn't exactly thirst for knowledge about the rest of the
family. What I did, finally, was put myself in the place of
Sam, wondering what Sam would feel if he were in the
room. I decided that Sam should be with Shlomo, that they
should see each other once more. I mean, here was his
long-lost brother, standing in my suite at the Hotel Ukraina
in the flesh, for God's sake! Of course, I knew that Sam
was both fascinated and horrified by the idea of going to
Russia—his usual ambivalence about things—but this was
simply too important. So I got on the telephone to Sam in
Brookline and I said, 'Look, I have your brother standing
here in this room. Talk to him.' They talked—Sam using a
few remembered words of Russian, Shlomo using a few
remembered words of Yiddish—and that conversation persuaded Sam to come to Russia after all."

At such a late date, it took a lot of string-pulling to get
him there. Because Sam had cancelled his visa and his
airline reservations, he was faced with the problem of having his travel documents reinstated on short notice. The
Russians were suspicious and wouldn't give a firm answer.
Higher influence was called for, and Lenny turned to, of
all people, Vice-President Richard Nixon. Lenny had met
Nixon the previous year during their coincidental good-will
tours of Latin America—Lenny's eliciting cheers, Nixon's
occasioning brickbats. (The irony of Nixon's interceding
on Sam's behalf was made all the sharper more than ten
years later, when Lenny's name appeared on President
Nixon's notorious "Enemies List.") But Nixon's pull
worked, and Sam, fresh visa in hand, left Boston for Paris
on September 8th.

At Orly Airport, where he changed planes for the flight
to Russia, Sam ran into Robert Saudek, a television producer who was also on his way to Moscow to film Lenny
and the Philharmonic for a TV special. "We sat together
on this Russian airliner," Saudek has recalled. "It was like

a 1900 Pullman car—rope hammocks overhead for small luggage, a lot of brass fixtures and worn carpeting. Sam was very nervous, very tense, and very talkative. He told me that he had eaten a big breakfast before he left Boston that morning, was served another big breakfast on the plane to Paris, then lunch, and as soon as we took off for Moscow we were presented with a huge Russian banquet. 'I have to accommodate them by eating what they offer,' Sam said, 'and I'm still accommodating.' He was stuffed but afraid to refuse anything—out of nervousness, I suppose. He confided how worried he was about going back to Russia. He had grave reservations about what was ahead— meeting his brother and nephew. His voice trembled when he talked about it. There was no sense of nostalgia or tingling excitement—just a kind of dread. Sometimes he spoke like a superpatriot, saying how wonderful America had been to him and how awful Russia was. As we came in for a landing at the Moscow airport, he almost seemed to be in shock. Felicia and Lenny were at the airport to meet him, and one of the first questions Lenny asked him was 'Do you want something to eat?' 'No!' Sam shouted."

In New York, I received a postcard from Sam, dated September 9th: "I arrived safe and happy. Lenny and Felicia met me at airport. I am being treated royalty. *Wotka* is my natural drink now. I love it. All my love, Dad." But not a word about Shlomo and Mikhoel, the real reasons for his anguished journey. And in a letter to my mother he just barely mentioned them. "Best regards from my brother and nephew," he wrote at the bottom of the page. Jennie, Shirley, and I, holding down the home front and expecting dramatic details of the great reunion, were perplexed. What was going on over there?

What was going on, it emerged later, was a large anticlimax. The two brothers were at last brought face to face. They collided with bear hugs, their eyes glistening, and then, according to Lenny, "they had absolutely nothing to

say to each other." Nothing. "There was a language bar-
rier, of course," Lenny has said, "but even through trans-
lators they hardly talked. I had to run off to a rehearsal, so
I didn't see the entire reunion, but I remember them being
very tentative, as if they were slightly afraid of each other.
Sam seemed to hit it off with Mikhoel, though. They talked
for a long time in Yiddish. But with Sam and Shlomo there
was no common ground."

The unexpected coolness between the brothers dis-
heartened Lenny, but it didn't surprise Hans Tuch, who
was the cultural attaché at the United States Embassy in
Moscow then. "Lenny kept commenting on how distant
the two brothers were," Tuch has recalled. "He brooded
about it a lot. But sometimes the distance between people
of opposing cultures can't be overcome, even if they are
blood brothers. I saw the same thing happen when George
Balanchine met his brother, who has stayed in Russia, after
many years." Robert Saudek and his associate, Mary
Ahern, also noticed the stiffness between Sam and
Shlomo, at a meal in the Ukraina dining room. "It wasn't
until the brother showed us his internal passport marked
'Jew,' that any real conversation took place," Mary Ahern
has said. "Sam and Lenny were shocked. I remember that
Lenny said, 'What would have happened if I'd grown up
here?' "

As the days passed in Moscow, Sam became more concerned with Lenny's concerts than with his relatives. Also,
Felicia had succeeded in tracking down Boris Pasternak,
the out-of-official-favor Nobel Prize novelist, in his village
outside Moscow. She brought Pasternak together with
Lenny, and she created a scandal throughout Russia by
inviting the author to a concert. In a way, the historical
novelist overshadowed the historical novel. When it was
nearly time for the touring Americans to leave Russia, on
September 12th, Lenny asked Sam if he would like to have
his visa extended, so he could visit longer with his relatives

and so some sightseeing. Without a moment's hesitation, Sam declined. "Before I even got here, I already had enough Russia to last me a lifetime," he said. He could hardly wait to leave.

I telephoned my father soon after he arrived back in Boston to ask him what had happened. What was it like to see your brother? "Well, we went to Lenny's concert and we walked in Red Square and I took pictures," Sam answered. "My nephew's wife and son joined us one day." That's all? "That's all," he said. "I'm very tired. You'll see them in the pictures I took."

On the occasion of his seventy-fifth birthday, in 1967, Sam received two letters, one each from Mikhoel and Shlomo, in a single envelope. The letters were expressions of greeting and good wishes for Sam and his family, betraying just a hint or two about their lives in Russia. Mikhoel wrote, "There's nothing new here unless you count the fact that we've got a bit older. Our son is already working independently. In our eyes, he is a very good young man." And Shlomo wrote, "All is as it was here, except that our health has got worse and worse. The heart doesn't want to work as it did before." Later that year, another letter arrived from Mikhoel:

My Dear Uncle and your family, *Shalom!*

I have received your letter, for which I am very grateful to you. We are pleased that all is well with you. In connection with your fiftieth wedding anniversary, much *nachas* from children and grandchildren.

Several days ago I received a letter from Uncle Shlomo. He asks that we give you regards and best wishes.

Things are, bless God, not bad here for us. Therewith I close. We look forward to your letters.

Be greeted and kissed.

Your Mikhoel and Lena

Regards from our son.

That was the last communication from Russia until a few months ago. For two years, I had tried through every likely channel to establish contact with any living relatives in the Soviet Union; the State Department, the Russian Embassy in Washington, the International Red Cross, even a quasi-private Moscow law firm called Iniurcolleguia produced no substantial help. Then, as a last resort, my Soviet lawyers suggested that they place a classified advertisement in the national edition of *Izvestia*, inquiring about the existence of Shlomo/Semyon Bernstein and Mikhoel Zvainboim. Remarkably, the advertisement was answered by both of them. I dispatched a cable to Mikhoel, sending my greetings and asking a lot of biographical questions. Again remarkably, he responded with a long, warm letter. He wrote me that his job as a vulcanizer in the Dnepropetrovsk chemical factory permitted him to retire in 1976, at age fifty-five, but that he continues to work at light jobs. In 1977, he suffered a heart attack, but is fairly healthy now. His wife, Lena, died in 1980, however—"my second grave loss, after the death of my parents and brothers." His son, Aleksandr, is a telemechanical engineer. Aleksandr married a woman named Sonia, also an engineer, in 1974, and they have two children—a daughter, Lena, and a son, Igor.

As for Shlomo ("Uncle Seme," Mikhoel calls him), he retired in 1955, at age fifty, and occupied himself with gardening on a small plot of land in Novosibirsk. His wife, Fanye, died in 1979, and now he lives in an apartment in Alma-Ata, near the Chinese border. "He is sick," Mikhoel wrote. "The last time he visited us was in 1974." Shlomo's son, also named Aleksandr, is a construction engineer, and a grandson is a student at an institute in Moscow.

In 1959, Uncle Seme, my wife, my child, and I met Uncle Samuel and Leonard in Moscow. The visit was unforgettable.

The Kids

That entire day remains fresh in my memory, among the happiest days of my life.

And I continue to meet with Leonard from afar, through his music, which runs through the entire movie "West Side Story." Our world champions in figure-skating, Rodnina and Zaitsev, did a performance to the music of Leonard. A Sunday television program, "Musical Kiosk," was dedicated to the work of Leonard. All this gives me reason to take pride in my cousin Leonard. . . . I wish you health, happiness, and the very best. Please write to me in detail about your life and all your relatives. Is Aunt Clara still alive? I'm at the end of my life. It would be nice to meet you. . . . My son, his family, and Uncle Seme send their regards.

I hug and kiss you.

Yours,
MIKHOEL

*A*T HIS JANUARY 7, 1962, testimonial dinner at the Sheraton Plaza in Boston, Sam was—as demonstrated by the lone group photograph I have of my family and me, just before that event—supremely ambivalent: he was being honored by officialdom, friends, and relatives for his seventy years of life and good works, and he was, as Jennie had put it, "on Cloud Ninety;" at the same time, the event marked the conclusion of his Biblical span, and, in his mind, every moment thenceforward would be borrowed from God. With an eerie expression of both glee and fear on his face, he enjoyed and suffered the long program—the playing of the national anthem by a small combo of patent *klezmers* (once, he had imagined his older son in such a group of struggling musicians, tinkling the ivories), the invocation, the saying of grace, the predictable chicken dinner, the greetings from the Mayor, the Massachusetts Attorney General, the head rabbi of the Boston Lubavitz Yeshiva, and then the scheduled "remarks" by various relatives and friends.

Despite a bad attack of flu, I had written out my remarks the day before. It was a difficult chore. How does one praise one's father, the man one knows too well? What is there to say beyond banality? Under the influence of a high fever, what I wrote, and later spoke, was, in part, this:

There aren't many of you here tonight who can claim you've known Samuel J. Bernstein for thirty years. Well, I have—and on fairly intimate terms—and may I say it's been and continues to be a thoroughly thrilling and rewarding experience. This is not meant facetiously. Few sons have had a father who offers so many charming surprises and kindnesses, so many moments of truth and integrity, so many spiritual and material gifts.

Those of you who have not known him for any great length of time probably think of him as basically a successful businessman who dabbles in various good causes—a man who has realized the classic American Dream, in the best Horatio Alger tradition, and has risen from the dingy herring bins of the Fulton Fish Market to an upstanding place in the Boston mercantile and religious communities. Well, that was pretty much how I thought of him until one day when I was about eight years old. We were playing his favorite, and rather primitive, game of stick-hurling in the back yard of our old summer house in Sharon when suddenly it began to rain. We repaired to the protection of an enormous oak tree and, within moments, my father had gratuitously embarked on an exacting discussion of a fine point of Talmudic logic, every bit as though he were talking with an intellectual equal. I sat back against the tree confused and entranced—not only by the intellectual calisthenics of it all but by the way my father went on, unsparing in his wealth of philosophical information, despite the fact that he was addressing an audience consisting of a very average eight-year-old boy and an oak tree. Quite frankly, I understood about one word in five, but that's not the point. The point is that I was the recipient of one of the rarest privileges a child can have—to be instructed by someone who truly loves to instruct. . . .

As I grew older, this didactic streak in my father lengthened and widened. I began to question him and eventually even argue with him, much as a student might do with his favorite professor. Then, one day, the essence of it all became alarmingly clear to me: Samuel J. Bernstein had missed his calling. He was not just a businessman—albeit a good one—he was a professor. A professor without a classroom. A man with a bottomless fund of information and opinion, who deeply loves to share it with others —and, what's more, has a native talent for doing so. . . . One must pay homage to such a rare man, and that is precisely what we are doing here tonight. And as a still confused but entranced son, I want to say to my father at this happy time, "Thank you and happy birthday."

Shirley was also called upon to speak in praise of her father, and although we had not discussed beforehand what we were going to say, she alluded to that same quality of Sam's—his love of learning and teaching. Then it was Lenny's turn. Amazingly, his words—again, without any prearrangement—touched on Sam's didacticism. "The greatest gift my father bestowed on me was to teach me to love learning," Lenny said. "He made it impossible for his children *not* to love learning." As a special tribute, Lenny played a piece he had written for the occasion, titled "Meditation on a Prayerful Theme My Father Sang in the Shower Thirty Years Ago." The shower theme was a Hasidic ditty that Sam liked, and Lenny explained that thirty years before he himself had performed variations on the theme "in the style of the great masters" as one of his musical tricks at a Mishkan Tefila Brotherhood dinner. "Tonight, in honor of my father, I play it in my own style," he said. The performance moved the honored father most of all. In his response, Sam said that his life had been a happy one, because his family had love for one another. It was true. A tenacious love was there, in spite of everything. The family was stronger than the sum of its fallible parts.

As Sam had feared, his physical health deteriorated after his three score years and ten. Circulation problems in his legs were followed by angina pains, which, in turn, were followed by prescribed medication that upset his stomach and his equilibrium. The cycle was completed by his heightened anxiety and depression, which aggravated his physical ailments. He stayed home from his office for weeks at a time, and began negotiations for the sale of his business. Whenever I saw him, he would say, "I'm as good as finished." Sam's decline was as hard on Jennie as it was on him. He rarely felt up to leaving the security of his house, even to see his grandchildren. The slightest untoward circumstance made him miserable. And caring for a semi-invalid weakened Jennie. (Sam couldn't abide a practical nurse around him.) Jennie began to experience angina pains herself. Then, in the spring of 1964, Sam found himself in an emergency situation. A nearly ruptured aneurysm of his aorta was discovered, and he was rushed to the Massachusetts General Hospital for surgery. He fully understood the gravity of the procedure—the replacement of his ravaged aorta with an Orlon prosthesis—and he was surprisingly calm about it. The night before the operation, he had a dream in which two angels argued over his fate. Finally, the pro-Sam angel won out, promising him a few more years of life. "I wasn't worried, because I knew I'd make it from my dream," Sam told me after his surgery.

Indeed, as his dream had foretold, he did have a few more years of life—five more—but there were days when he wished that the anti-Sam angel had won. His arteries further degenerated, and the pain was sometimes unbear-

able. In November of 1966, he and Jennie flew to New York
to spend Thanksgiving with their family. When I picked
them up, at LaGuardia Airport, I was appalled at how frail
and waxen Sam had become in the few weeks since I had
seen him last. New York was undergoing a weird spell of
summerlike weather, with an accompanying temperature
inversion and smog. You could taste the air, and the taste
was that of burnt rubber. As soon as Sam arrived, he complained of dizziness and nausea. That night, he had a
crushing heart attack. He survived, returning to Boston
three weeks later, but from then on it was a grim cycle of
more cardiac incidents, longer hospitalizations, and, during his last year, nurses around the clock, whether he cared
for their presence or not. His lingering, tenuous hold on
life ended at Boston's Beth Israel Hospital on April 30,
1969, with Jennie at his bedside. He died just a few months
short of seeing the astronauts land on the moon. It would
have been a fine conclusion for a life that began with his
marvelling at the speed of a kulak's droshky. The funeral
was a sombre version of the testimonial dinner seven years
earlier. As he was buried, alongside his mother and father,
flocks of disparate people came once again to pay homage
to the man—an extraordinary man, for all that.

Sam's terminal decline and death almost did Jennie in,
too. Even with round-the-clock nurses attending her husband, Jennie was never more than a few steps away from
the sickbed. Only she could make tea just the way he liked
it, only she knew how many banana slices he preferred on
his Cream of Wheat, only she understood what he meant
when he said, "My legs are drawing." For a while, she was
popping almost as many nitroglycerin pills as he was, but,
despite our urgent pleas, she wouldn't relax her ministra-
tions to the man with whom she had lived for fifty-two
years, for better for worse. As a marriage, it had been more
of the latter than the former, but Jennie had taken that

nuptial injunction seriously and stuck it out. After Sam died and the first shock of mourning and loneliness began to dissipate, she tended to expunge from her memory all the unhappy moments of the fifty-two years, and she spoke of Sam only as a hero, a devoted husband, a great provider.

Before long, a new Jennie was revealed to her kids. We had always known that she was a tough lady, a survivor, but as a widow she showed a different sort of mettle—a plucky independence. She discovered herself and came into her own at last, easily replacing Sam as the cynosure of the family. In Newton, where she lives—near her sisters Dorothy and Bertha (Betty had died in 1961)—she is the darling of her new set of friends, most of whom are involved in the local art scene and would have been deplored by Sam. She attends concerts, museum openings, theatre, ballet, and "functions and affairs galore." (As Jennie put it recently, "I like to keep adrift of things.") She travels, too, as much as her age and health will allow. Her life, in its eighty-fifth year, is full and truly liberated, in the best sense of the term.

My continuing collection of Jenniana also shows a change. In her station as the doyenne of the family and the living parent of Leonard Bernstein, she has developed an awareness of her position that can be, at times, just a hair cavalier. A few years ago, when the producers of "60 Minutes" asked her to be interviewed on camera for a television piece they were doing on Lenny, she rejected the invitation out of hand. "I don't need that kind of publicity," she said. Recently, she has tended to refer to her celebrated son as "Leonard," even when she is talking about him with old friends or relatives. "Why do you call him 'Leonard' when you're talking to me, of all people?" Shirley once wondered aloud, with a touch of amused annoyance. Jennie replied, "Do you *mind* if I call him 'Leonard'? It's his name, isn't it?"

The Kids

When my father was sick and failing, he entered into painful negotiations for the sale of his business. We had a long talk about it one day, and Sam was in a reflective mood. "You know," he said, rocking his wrists to adjust his shirt cuffs—the gesture that meant the start of a discourse—"it's a big disappointment to me that none of you kids wanted to take over the business and live in Boston. But when I think about it all the younger generations in the Bernstein family went against their parents' wishes. My grandfather, Bezalel, became a blacksmith instead of a rabbi like his father. My father became a rabbi instead of a blacksmith. I ran away from the *shtetl* to be a businessman in America. Now my own kids won't have anything to do with my work and my life. We're a funny family that way. Who knows what your kids and Lenny's will turn out to be?"

This matter of occupational rebellion came up at a Thanksgiving dinner not long ago. The latest generation of Bernsteins agreed that they had revolted against their respective parents' work, but, strangely, they all have since become attracted to artistic pursuits—especially performing. Lenny's son, Alexander, who, at twenty-six, is now trying to become an actor, said, "Those musicians and writers and so on who were around the house when we were growing up suddenly seemed more interesting—or less boring—than other people. I guess we want to be like them." Apparently, the generation gap has narrowed, with more similarity of culture, language, tastes, and education —although I notice that our kids have their private mockeries of their parents. In fact, Lenny's daughter Jamie has been keeping a journal, and I fear it is not unlike my collection of parental data. That's how it goes. And it serves us right.

Perhaps Lenny, Shirley, and I were educated too much and grew too worldly. We patronized and ridiculed our less educated, less worldly parents. We had it too easy. It's a common enough American experience with offspring of immigrants. But throughout our guilt-ridden discomfort with our parents, arrogant derision of them, and our final acceptance of them, there was always love. To our credit, we never denied or apologized. The family was the family, after all. Whether we like it or not, we are the living aggregates of all those old genes and acquired characteristics. It's the nature of things. And when it comes to the nature of things, one can only hope for the best. As Sam used to say, "Keep your finger crossed."

Epilogue

Throughout the 1980s, since the writing and publication of "Family Matters," the Bernsteins had pretty much done what I suggested on the last page of the book: As far as the nature of things was concerned, we hoped for the best and—pace Sam—kept our collective finger crossed. The formula worked magically well. Our situations in the nature of things stayed the same or got better. We dared not say it aloud, or even think it, but we seemed to be blessed, knock wood, *kinahora*, *inshallah*, please God.

First and foremost, of course, there was Lenny. The 1980s witnessed his emergence as a mature, revered artist. Those snappish tribes of pompous critics and envious musicians and dubious concert-goers suddenly decided—en masse, it appeared—that Lenny was a little too old and renowned to be just that eternally charming, brilliant flash-in-the-pan. Hell, even his talented disciples were getting a bit long in the tooth. All at once, Lenny's interpretations of, say, Mahler swelled to the stuff of legend, like Toscanini's Beethoven or Koussevitzky's Tchaikovsky. He was no longer an aging *Wunderkind* but an authentic, original, and—still incredible—a born-and-bred *American* maestro. He was, in truth and at long last, what Shirley and I used to kid him about—a veritable *chef d'orchestre distingué*. Of course, for all the glowing hosannas and honors and honorariums, he was still our "Lennuhtt," albeit a trifle less nimble on the tennis court. And he was still what made us tick as the singular, inseparable Bernstein family.

As for Jennie—the mother of us all, the dowager queen—she burst into her nineties with a vengeance against the inevitables and with a renewed thirst for life. Her body may have been frailer but her mind, if anything, was keener. She gloried in her family and luxuriated in Lenny's increasing celebrity. At his somewhat excessive world-televised seventieth birthday party at Tanglewood in August of 1988, she was almost as much the cynosure as the honored maestro himself and she was cheered as heartily. She loved every second of it, and stayed on until the very end of the party in the small hours of the morning. Even the deaths of her younger sisters Bertha and Dorothy did not depress her for too long. Her resilience was astounding.

And new pages were continually added to "The Jennie Bernstein Cookbook." For instance, just before her ninetieth birthday, Jennie was told by a friend that she was about to experience a momentous event most people will never experience. "I know," Jennie replied reflectively. "It's a once-in-a-lifetime affair." She admitted that she was "on tentacles" about the occasion. Not long after that unique affair, she was asked how she was feeling. "O.K., but in the morning I'm a little blasé." My daughter, Karen, was at one point working for an organization helping the Boston homeless, and she described to her grandmother how serious the problem was. "You wouldn't know the half of it," Jennie said. "You don't watch it on TV, like I do." And when I was about to embark on an August vacation to Cape Cod, I expressed the hope that one of those three-day fogs wouldn't spoil things, to which Jennie mused, "Yes, that fog comes in on little padded toes." (Actually, now that I think of it, her version may be an improvement on Sandburg.) When Lenny conducted Beethoven's Ninth in Berlin as the notorious wall dividing that city crumbled, Jennie anointed him "my prince of peace." She had also proclaimed that "he's not just an artist—he's a regular celebrity." Yet when he played her a slightly abstruse selection from his "Songfest," she cautioned him that it was better to write "nice tunes people like to hear." And when he was in Boston to visit at Harvard for some reason, Jennie wondered grumpily, "So what prizes are they going to give you now—some Pulitzers?" As Jennie herself often said in moments of self-depreciation, "You know, I'm not getting any younger. I'm no longer the girl I used to be."

Shirley, like her mother and every other mortal, was not getting any younger, either. But it was her nature to be an eternal girl—in spirit, in her professional life as a respected and successful agent, in her capacities as a loyal and loving daughter, sister, aunt, and friend.

And as for Shirley's nieces and nephews—Lenny's kids Jamie, Alexander, and Nina, and my kids Karen and Michael—the past decade saw them all enter adulthood as reasonably educated, responsible, healthy, generous, handsome, and decent people, which is certainly an unalloyed blessing, considering that outrageous decade. The eldest, Jamie, was married in 1984 to David Thomas, once her classmate at Harvard, and now a distinguished marketing executive. She composes startlingly good songs and performs them with dash, and she is a cultural commentator, but her true forte turned out to be motherhood. Francisca ("Frankie") Thomas was born in 1987 and Evan Samuel came along in 1989, thrilling everybody, but nobody more than Jamie herself. Both Alexander and Nina spent some years trying to be actors in an actor-saturated world. They finally adopted far more rewarding occupations; Alexander took to teaching and Nina to gourmet catering. Lenny couldn't have been more proud of the three of them—and, probably, more relieved.

Both the mother and father of Karen and Michael were proud and relieved, too. Karen and Michael were gainfully employed—she as a television producer, and he as an arts administrator—and happy they are to be so in their chosen fields. Ellen and I have each remarried; Ellen to the Australian journalist Ian Ball, and I, to Jane Anderson, a fiction editor.

Things have worked out nicely all around—even for the

surviving Russian relatives, comparatively speaking. We kept in touch with them throughout the promising glasnost-per-estroika Gorbachev years, and in 1988, when Lenny led an international youth orchestra on a Russian tour, he met with our cousin Mikhoel Zvainboim and his family and Uncle Shlomo's son, Aleksandr. Since then, Mikhoel, before he died recently, reported that he, his son, daughter-in-law, and grandchildren had visited a cousin in Israel, which was "like a wonderful dream." Uncle Shlomo, elderly and quite frail, is a lonely widower now living with his son in Moscow. According to his son, he remains a disciplined, self-reliant, dedicated Russian patriot who reached "old age with honor." My uncle wrote me to say that he has few complaints and even has some rubles put aside "for a rainy day and my funeral." Aleksandr earned an early retirement from his profession as a hydroelectric engineer in the Yakutia (the extreme north), where he worked for more than twenty years.

So the 1980s were, by and large, kind to the Bernsteins. But then came the 1990s. In April, 1990, Lenny was diagnosed as suffering from inoperable lung cancer, and everything changed drastically for each of us, just as it had in November, 1943, when Lenny made his spectacular début in Carnegie Hall.

I suppose, in retrospect, the diagnosis wasn't an enormous surprise to me. Lenny, from day one of his life, was a puny, wheezy asthmatic—he suffered from "a weak chest, like his father," Jennie often said—and his chronic asthma and emphysema kept him out of military service during the Second World War. And, as all the world knew and rued, he was rarely without a lit cigarette in hand or mouth; he ingested cigarette smoke as if it were pure, life-sustaining oxygen. In a lethally perverse way, it was life-sustaining to him; he claimed that he was incapable of thinking or creating or performing without inhaling the accursed nicotine, he was that addicted. Of course, he knew full well the peril of such addiction; just twelve years before the crushing diagnosis, his beloved wife, Felicia, an equally heavy smoker, died of metastasized lung cancer, and numerous friends had come to untimely ends from smoking over the years. Lenny lectured himself and every other smoker about quitting "the goddam things," and he was awed and elated when others actually succeeded in kicking the habit, but although he tried to stop many times he always failed. Now, at long last, his body was failing him.

The doctors' prognosis of their diagnosis was not good. They treated him with the best therapies that medical science had to offer, at the best medical institutions—where he was registered as one "Carlo Levi," a mysterious reference to the Italian writer. (I have since anagrammed "Carlo Levi" in search of an encoded clue to Lenny's feelings at the time, but all I've come up with is "clear viol," "evil carol," and "ill over a C.") The medicine men provided him with many tiny handles of hope, none of which was, alas, attached to anything substantial. It was a crazy free fall: Lenny—although he denied it for many months, even fulfilling ruinous concert engagements in Czechoslovakia and Japan and, finally, at Tanglewood—knew it in his heart of hearts. His children, Shirley and I knew it, too. The ghastly news was slowly leaking around the world as rumor and half-truth despite our fervent attempts to keep the whole truth secret, especially from Jennie.

But you couldn't keep the whole truth from a consummate mother who had spent seventy-two of her ninety-two years on this earth caring for and adoring her first-born. She, of course, knew him better than anyone, and she could sniff out the seriousness of his illness even over the telephone. To ease her constant concern, Lenny promised her that he had stopped smoking for good—a blatant white lie,

compounded by a proffered engraved gold plate attesting to
the pale whopper—and he continued to tell her what he told
the world, that he was recovering from a combination of
exhaustion and pneumonia. But Jennie, always the intuitive
mother, intuited the truth and tried to confirm it through
her constant grilling of Shirley and me. We denied all her
suspicions, not fooling her for a minute. During one call to
Shirley, she cried in despair about Lenny, "We're more than
mother and son, we grew up together!"—which, like so
many of Jennie's more famous lines, smacks of an essential
verity. And at age ninety-two, as she learned more and more
about Lenny's inevitable decline, she confided, "This is taking years off my life."

Throughout the spring and summer of 1990, Lenny's
state of health occupied almost all our thoughts and actions;
we seemed incapable of doing anything that wasn't somehow connected to Lenny and his rapidly worsening condition. It was an extended bad dream of hushed conferences
with doctors, chilling visits to hospitals, and clumsy
attempts at pretending it was family life as usual. Then, on
August 19th, it all came to an extraordinarily beautiful and,
at once, ghastly climax at Tanglewood, in a way the most apt
setting for such an event. Only Lenny and those of us closest
to him knew, with a fair degree of certainty, that his Sunday
afternoon concert with the Boston Symphony Orchestra
would be his farewell performance. Before the first note had
sounded, however, that awful probability became apparent
to the general audience, as well. A notice was placed in the
program booklet stating that Lenny's most recent composition, "Arias and Barcarolles," would be led by the Boston
Symphony's assistant conductor, Carl St. Clair, so that the
maestro's energy could be conserved for Benjamin Britton's
"Four Sea Interludes from Peter Grimes" and Beethoven's
Seventh Symphony.

A joyless murmuring suffused the Tanglewood Shed as

we awaited Lenny's appearance on stage. Even the weather contributed to the sense of foreboding. Over the decades, Lenny unfailingly had enjoyed what came to be called "Bernstein weather" for his Tanglewood concerts—warm, clear skies that attracted lawns full of music-lovers, picnic-lovers, and/or just plain lovers—but that Sunday afternoon in August of 1990 was cold, damp, and dismally November-gray. Hardly a soul braved the wet lawn, although the Shed was packed. When Lenny—hunched, spindly, gray as the sky, and suddenly looking too small for his afternoon-formal white jacket, he whose solid torso had always seemed to be bursting the seams of his conducting attire—shuffled gamely to the podium, a barely perceptible gasp of disbelief preceded the welcoming ovation. He was obviously no longer the vital, bouncy Lenny that Tanglewood audiences had so long adored. Our family and his staff knew that he was able to go on only with the aid of powerful bronchial-dilator sprays and an oxygen dispenser backstage. With all that, the concert was definitive and unforgettable. Britten's pieces from "Peter Grimes" were, Lenny had told me earlier, programmed partly in my honor, of all things, since I had worked at Tanglewood, in the summer of 1946, as a 14-year-old lighting technician for the opera's American première and had come to learn the thing by heart. His playing of the interludes was wrenching nostalgia for both of us, and his playing of Beethoven's Seventh was the best I had ever heard, despite the obvious pain he was in and the hacking, helpless coughing fits that all but left the orchestra to its own devices for several heart-stopping moments. The ovations at the end of the concert were nothing short of hysterical. Jennie, who was ensconced backstage in the heated green room because of the dank conditions in the Shed, saw Lenny stagger through the concert, sucking on oxygen tubes and dilators at every opportunity, and her darkest suspicions were confirmed: she would most likely outlive her first-born son, which was against the natural order of things.

From then on, little by little, it was announced that various planned appearances by Lenny throughout the world were either postponed or cancelled outright. The indelicate peppered us with questions; the more judicious merely avoided the subject of Lenny's health entirely. The world's press continued to speculate, occasionally coming up with something approaching the truth of the matter. Finally, on October 9, 1990, it was announced that Lenny was retiring from the concert stage because of poor health and would devote his remaining time to composing, writing, and education. The shock of this news hit everyone hard—from the loftiest musician to a cashier in my local supermarket whose children had grown up watching Lenny on TV ("I'm praying for your brother," she told me, patting my arm).

As for Lenny himself, he seemed to disintegrate before one's very eyes. It still pains me to describe in any detail the excruciating despair of his last weeks on this earth. Suffice it to say that once the final tiny handle of hope had slipped away, we all wished for a swift, quiet end—wished for it with that terrible access of humane logic which often envelops a loving, close family faced with the certain, imminent death of one of its own. The end came on Sunday evening, October 14th, just five days after the shocking retirement announcement. Lenny's great heart simply gave out.

No one had to remind the devastated Bernstein family of the magnitude of its, and the world's, loss, but none of us was really prepared for the extraordinary outpouring of grief from all over. For instance, the New York *Daily News*—which had in 1943 compared Lenny's last-minute substitution for Bruno Walter to "a shoestring catch in center field"—outshone its competition with an eloquent full-front-page photograph, bordered in black and bearing the simple legend "LEONARD BERNSTEIN (1918-1990)."

Cities and nations where Lenny had been adopted as a native son—including even Germany (Germany!)—lowered their flags to half-staff and declared periods of mourning. (For reasons best known to the Bush Administration, the United States of America was not among them.) And of the thousands of condolence notes the family received, none was more touching than the letter from the total stranger, who invariably wrote, "You don't know me but I just had to say how sorry I am to somebody close to him." Memorial events followed one after the other, with the Carnegie Hall concert a month after his death instantly becoming mythic.

For me, the absolute proof of what Lenny meant to the disparate reaches of the world took place during the funeral cortege to the Greenwood Cemetery in Brooklyn, where he was to be buried beside Felicia. The long line of black limousines, led by the hearse and a phalanx of New York's finest on wailing motorcycles, came to an unexpected stop at the eastern exit of an East River tunnel. Other traffic was also halted at a nearby construction site, and while the essentially New York cross section of motorists, pedestrians, and construction workers waited for things to move again, they stood in the matchless warm sunlight and stared at the stalled cortege, while we in the limos stared blankly back. After several minutes of this strange stalemate, the motorcycles wailed anew and the funeral procession began to roll again. The onlookers—Hispanic and Oriental mothers holding up their children and Orthodox Jews huddling together and students with backpacks and cab drivers leaning on their open doors and a legion of white, black, and brown hardhats—suddenly shouted as if on cue, "Good-bye, Lenny, good-bye!" If it were a scene filmed for a 1950s Warner Brothers movie, it probably would have ended up on the cutting-room floor. But it wasn't; it was real life and it was the finest tribute of them all, the one that would have made Lenny most proud.

A few hours earlier that day, at the crowded private funeral service in Lenny's cavernous apartment on Central Park West, I delivered my own tribute, which I had written almost immediately after his death as a kind of therapy. The eulogy was as follows:

My brother Lenny, who was always larger than life, turned out to be smaller than death. Amazingly—just like that!—he is no more. It seems impossible.

Those of us who were closest to him, who knew him best and longest, who loved him most, we—such lucky ones we are!—we somehow assumed that he would go on forever, like time itself, that he was somehow immortal, not just perishable matter like the rest of us.

There would, we felt, always be our Lenny doing what he did so passionately, so brilliantly, so charmingly, so originally, so lovingly, and, yes, sometimes so excessively—always so full of life and so much larger than life.

All the world knows what he did:

Teaching people—his favorite occupation, really. Descended from rabbis, he was a rabbi at heart, a master teacher. Just listening to Lenny was an education. (I know this better than most because I was taught by Lenny from just about my first day on this earth.) There was nothing he'd rather do than stimulate new thoughts for, especially, young minds.

Making history. He *was* the living precedent for American music—the first American to be taken seriously on the concert stage. I think it can be said that he made it possible for any talented American kid to follow in his footsteps.

Experimenting with the new, even though he was a hopeless traditionalist. He welcomed the avant-garde, but he cherished the pristine, lovely tune—the simple song.

Revivifying the old—which I believe was his greatest gift as a conductor. How often have we heard, as if for the first time, an *echt* Lenny rendition of, say, Tchaikovsky's Fifth or Brahm's First, and marveled at all the nuances we had missed over the years? How often have we seen and listened to him draw, through sheer love and musicianly example, unforgettable performances from orchestras—performances the musicians would later admit that they never knew they had in them? His very last concert—conducting Beethoven's Seventh at Tanglewood—was only the most recent case in point.

Preaching love and peace. Naïvely, he wanted the whole world to love itself into one big happy family, and he took it as a personal affront when the world refused to comply. He maintained unflinching optimism and religious trust in the ultimate improvability of man, despite all the hard evidence to the contrary. Lenny was in love with love.

Helping young talent and his less celebrated, less lucky contemporaries, some of whom responded to his kindnesses with rank envy and disloyalty, which, typically, Lenny was quick to ignore or forgive.

And for those of us who were his nearest and dearest, there will always be the special memories:

His love of games, and particularly, his infuriating success in trouncing us at anagrams—the game of games, at least to him. And then there were tennis and squash and skiing and swimming and sailing and touch football—the last featuring the annual Thanksgiving classic, called the Nose Bowl, in the backyard of his house in Fairfield, Connecticut.

His grand generosity with his worldly goods and with his loving spirit. No one in Lenny's company was ever left wanting. And a compliment from Lenny was like no other compliment; it was total, absolute, and thoroughly thrilling for the fortunate recipient. (Of course, he could also be occasionally tactless. Shirley once said that if you happened to have a pimple on the end of your nose, Lenny would lose no time in pointing it out to you—and perhaps the entire world. He was an *enfant terible* to the end.)

His happiness at others' happiness. He really did share in others' joy, and also in their grief.

His "obliging at the pianoforte," as he would put it—at Thanksgiving, Christmas, birthdays, Passover, whatever, whenever, great occasion or not.

His humor, which so often went with the "obliging." A great joke was a great performance for Lenny. He could laugh—and make us all laugh—in a dozen languages, including our very own private family language called Rybernian. Language: To Lenny, words were mysterious, astonishing creatures—to be scrutinized and analyzed like cells under a microscope. Words were the equals of musical notes for him, and he loved them with equal fervor. One of the last conversations we had together was about handling words. "I'm a pretty good editor," he said, simply—and proudly.

All those things that were Lenny are no more, and that terrible fact is unbelievable and unbearable. For my part, I miss him more than I can ever say. He was my brother, my best friend, and a sort of father, too. Whatever I am, for better or worse, I owe to Lenny. And a lot of other kith and kin can say the same. He is irreplaceable for me and mine—and, I suspect, for you and yours, too.

And yet, of course, the great obvious cliché that springs to mind is quite true: Lenny is immortal, after all. The memories of him will be there, along with the recordings and the revivals and the writings, for generations upon generations. Just as long as people care a damn about something finer in life than power and money and their imagined superiority over others there will always be Lenny around to educate, entertain, edify, move and inspire—to change us all in some wonderful, subtle way.

Epilogue

In that sense, Lenny is larger than mere death, too.

Jennie lived on—as she conceded, not getting any younger and no longer the girl she used to be—and she was attended round-the-clock in her Newton apartment by devoted home-care aides. She often complained about gaps in her memory, but those devoted aides reported that nothing escaped her attention, including the subtleties of the Persian Gulf War. Then, on December 21, 1991, she had a moderate stroke, which mainly affected her speech. After she came home from the hospital, she was visited regularly by a therapist who succeeded only in irritating Jennie with nasty vocal exercises. At last, Jennie dismissed the poor woman and practiced speaking on her own. Soon, she was her old articulate, if malapropian, self—"a medical marvel," according to her doctor. She voted knowledgeably and sensibly in the 1992 elections. But exactly one year after her first stroke, she suffered a second, and this time massive, stroke. She never regained consciousness; her tough, mill-girl heart finally gave out eight days later, just a few months short of her 95th birthday. It was one hell of a life for the immigrant kid from Shepetovka.

Shirley, meanwhile, was not doing too well herself. Out of nowhere she was visited with a rare blood disease that, at first, was a minor distraction, but soon developed into prolonged deterioration of her body and spirit. She hung on doggedly until May 20, 1998, when her heart, every bit as game as Lenny's and her mother's, also gave out. Another burial at Greenwood, near Lenny and Felicia, and another eulogy for a beloved sibling. The eulogy concluded: "I choose to remember Shirley as that pretty, bright, funny kid shrieking operatic duets with Lenny until her vocal chords grew raw, struggling with piano versions of Beethoven symphonies on the ancient upright in our summer-house living room (she never had a formal piano lesson), giggling and gossiping with the Kaplan twins from across the street, and—most vividly for me—her nose in a book (as our mother always complained when there was housework to be done), twirling and twirling her forelock with her forefinger as she read, and occasionally munching a thick lettuce-and-tomato sandwich on white bread with mayonnaise—lots and lots of mayonnaise. What a kid! What a woman, that Shirl!"

As for us Bernstein survivors, we carry on. Jamie, Alexander, and Nina are ever more involved in the operation of their father's enterprises, known as the Amberson Group, Inc. ("Sam Bernstein's revenge," Dave Thomas described it). Alexander is happily married to the former Elizabeth Velazquez. They have a daughter, Anya. Nina is married to Rudd Simmons, a film producer. My offspring, Karen and Michael, are still gainfully employed in their chosen fields, and I—the long-term baby of the family and perennial kid brother—suddenly find myself the Family Elder, a heady role in which I must be available, in the unlikely event I'm ever called upon, for sage advice and good cheer.

That wondrous finger of Sam's is still firmly crossed.